Quality Code

Quality Code

Software Testing Principles, Practices, and Patterns

Stephen Vance

♠♦Addison-Wesley

Upper Saddle River, NJ • Boston • Indianapolis • San Francisco
New York • Toronto • Montreal • London • Munich • Paris • Madrid
Capetown • Sydney • Tokyo • Singapore • Mexico City

Many of the designations used by manufacturers and sellers to distinguish their products are claimed as trademarks. Where those designations appear in this book, and the publisher was aware of a trademark claim, the designations have been printed with initial capital letters or in all capitals.

The author and publisher have taken care in the preparation of this book, but make no expressed or implied warranty of any kind and assume no responsibility for errors or omissions. No liability is assumed for incidental or consequential damages in connection with or arising out of the use of the information or programs contained herein.

The publisher offers excellent discounts on this book when ordered in quantity for bulk purchases or special sales, which may include electronic versions and/or custom covers and content particular to your business, training goals, marketing focus, and branding interests. For more information, please contact:

U.S. Corporate and Government Sales
(800) 382-3419
corpsales@pearsontechgroup.com

For sales outside the United States, please contact:

International Sales
international@pearsoned.com

Visit us on the Web: informit.com/aw

Library of Congress Cataloging-in-Publication Data

Vance, Stephen.

Quality code : software testing principles, practices, and patterns / Stephen Vance.

pages   cm

Includes index.

ISBN 978-0-321-83298-6 (alk. paper)—ISBN 0-321-83298-1 (alk. paper)

1. Computer software—Testing. 2. Software patterns. I. Title. II. Title: Software testing principles, practices, and patterns.

QA76.76.T48V36 2013

005.1'4—dc23   2013036018

ISBN-13: 978-0-321-83298-6
ISBN-10:   0-321-83298-1

Text printed in the United States on recycled paper at RR Donnelley in Crawfordsville, Indiana.
First printing, November 2013

To my 자기야
for your continuous love and support.

To my parents
for preparing me for this and all other accomplishments.

———————————————

Contents

Preface

Lean production has revolutionized manufacturing over the last several decades. Frameworks like TQM, Just-In-Time, Theory of Constraints, and the Toyota Production System have vastly improved the general state of automotive and manufacturing quality and spawned a vital competitive landscape. The family of Agile software development approaches brings the principles of Lean production to the knowledge discipline of software product development, but it needs to adapt these principles to a less mechanical context.

The idea of building the quality into the product in order to increase customer satisfaction and reduce the overall lifetime cost of maintenance has resulted in practices like test-driven development (TDD) and other test-first and test-early approaches. Regardless of which flavor you espouse, you need to understand what testable software looks like and master a wide range of techniques for implementing tests to be successful. I have found the gap between the principles and the state of the practice is often an unacknowledged source of failure in testing regimens. It is easy to say "use test-driven development," but when faced with a project, many developers do not know where to start.

In showing people how to apply test-driven, or at least test-early, development, I often find that one of the obstacles is the mechanics of writing tests. Exercising a method as a mathematical function that purely translates inputs to easily accessible outputs is no problem. But much software has side effects, behavioral characteristics, or contextual constraints that are not as easy to test.

This book arose from a recurring need to show developers how to test the specific situations that stymied them. Consistently, we would sit down for a few minutes, we would write a unit test for the troublesome code, and the developer would have a new tool in his belt.

What Is This Book About?

This book is about easily and routinely testing all of your software. It primarily focuses on unit tests, but many of the techniques apply to higher-level tests as well. This book will give you the tools—the implementation patterns—to test almost any code and to recognize when the code needs to change to be testable.

What Are the Goals of This Book?

This book will help you

- Understand how to easily unit test all of your code
- Improve the testability of your software design
- Identify the applicable testing alternatives for your code
- And write tests in a way that will scale with the growth of your applications

  In support of these goals, this book provides you with

- Over two-dozen detailed techniques for testing your code with lots of examples
- Guidance on the right testing technique for a wide range of situations
- And an approach to unit testing that helps you focus your efforts

Who Should Read This Book?

This book is primarily written for the professional software developer and software developer in test who want to increase their skill at code-level testing as a means to improve the quality of their code. This book should be particularly useful to test-driven development (TDD) and test-early practitioners to help them ensure the correctness of their code from the start. Many of the techniques in this book also apply to integration and system testing.

What Background Do You Need?

This book assumes that the following points are true.

- You are sufficiently fluent in object-oriented languages to be able to read and understand examples in Java, C++, and other languages and apply them to your language of choice.

- You are familiar with concepts of code-level testing and xUnit framework members such as JUnit.

- You are conversant in or have ready reference to information on design patterns and refactoring.

What Is in This Book?

Part I (Chapters 1–5) covers the principles and practices that guide successful testing. Chapter 1 puts the approaches in the book into an engineering context, discussing engineering, craftsmanship, and first-time quality in general as well as some software-specific concerns. Chapter 2 examines the role of intent. Chapter 3 outlines an approach to testing to help you focus your efforts. Chapter 4 discusses the interaction between design and testability, including some thoughts on scaling your testing efforts. Chapter 5 presents a number of testing principles that you can use to guide your testing decisions.

Part II (Chapters 6–13) details the implementation patterns for testing, starting with bootstrapping your tests and the basic catalog of techniques in Chapter 6. Chapters 7 through 12 elaborate on the topics introduced in Chapter 6, with an interlude to investigate intent more deeply in Chapter 9. Chapter 13 takes a deep technical dive into what many people consider impossible by introducing techniques for deterministically reproducing race conditions.

Part III (Chapters 14 and 15) takes the principles and techniques from the rest of the book and provides a narrative for applying them in two real-life, worked examples. Chapter 14 examines using test-driven development to create a Java application from scratch, showing how to get started and how to apply the techniques in a strictly typed language. Chapter 15 takes an untested, open-source JavaScript jQuery plugin and brings it under test, demonstrating an approach to taming legacy code in a dynamic language. Both examples contain references to the detailed GitHub commit history behind the narrative.

Those Who Came Before

All advances build on the prior efforts of others. This work grew up in the context of a number of influences from the last fifteen years of computing. This list is not exhaustive, and I hope I do not offend those whom I missed or who did not receive as much publicity, but I would like to call out

- The influencers and signatories of the Agile Manifesto
- The pioneers of early Agile development approaches, such as Kent Beck with eXtreme Programming
- The Gang of Four and Martin Fowler for design patterns and refactoring
- The software craftsmanship movement and Robert C. "Uncle Bob" Martin
- More recent seminal work in software testing by Michael Feathers and Gerard Meszaros

I have had the good fortune to work with several of the colleagues of these luminaries from their formative teams.

Acknowledgments

All authors say that they could not have written their books without the support of their partners in life. I did not appreciate the full meaning of that until going through the process myself. I really could not have brought this book to fruition without the continual support and encouragement of my wife, Jenny, from her patience with the time investment to the daily statement of, "I'll clean up dinner. You go write."

I would like to thank Greg Doench for his patience with a first-time author and his experienced guidance through the editorial process. The review feedback of Zee Spencer, Eric E. Meyer, and Jerry Eshbaugh helped me focus and refine the material to its current form; I hope I did their feedback justice.

Trent Richardson, author of the jQuery Timepicker Addon used as the subject of the worked example in Chapter 15, has been wonderfully enthusiastic and supportive of the efforts to bring the project under test. He has accepted all pull requests to date. As of this writing, the first release with tests just went live.

I have had the opportunity to coach and manage several teams over the years. You do not really know something until you know how to teach it. You all know who you are. Thank you for being my reason to grow.

The authors of many articles in *Dr. Dobbs' Journal* and *Software Development* magazine stimulated my early thinking on test-early approaches. Eric E. Meyer, Jean-Pierre Lejacq, and Ken Faw showed me the disciplined ways of TDD. Many of my formative opportunities occurred with or through Christopher Beale. Our careers have intertwined, including our work with Joe Dionise; much of my early design and architecture experience was forged under their mentorship.

Finally, two professors have unknowingly had a strong influence that culminated in this book. Professor Lee, formerly of the University of Michigan in the early 1990s, showed me that computer science could be more than just a hobby. In my first class of my master's program, Professor Janusz Laski of Oakland University introduced me to formal verification and static and dynamic analysis methods, instrumental in my understanding and advocacy of tools to support the software-development process.

About the Author

Stephen Vance has been a professional software developer, consultant, manager, mentor, and instructor since 1992. He has practiced and taught code-level, automated testing techniques since 1997. He has worked across a broad range of industries for companies ranging from start-ups to Fortune 100 corporations. He has spoken at software conferences throughout the United States and Europe. Stephen lives with his wife near Boston, Massachusetts.

Part I

Principles and Practices of Testing

Testing, in particular automated tests written in code, pervades software engineering. Whether through test-driven development, continuous integration, behavior-driven development, continuous delivery, acceptance test-driven development, specification by example, integration testing, system testing, or unit testing, everyone involved in software-based product development has a chance to write automated tests. Agile, Lean,[1] and software craftsmanship movements

---

1. I use Lean to refer to a Lean Production approach derived from the Lean Manufacturing movement as opposed to Lean Startup. The opinions about quality in this chapter apply to the sustainably productized software you need after you have learned what works from your Lean Startup experiments, if that is your business approach.

espouse high levels of testing to support rapid development and high quality.

Thought leaders in software engineering promote code-based testing as an essential part of the professional developer's repertoire. "Uncle Bob" Martin [CC08, CC11] espouses it for software craftsmanship. Gerard Meszaros [xTP] consolidates the lexicon around it. Steve Freeman and Nat Pryce [GOOS] describe how to grow your software with a healthy dose of testing. Michael Feathers [WEwLC] shows you how to rescue your old code through testing and even defines legacy code as code without tests. Kent Beck [XPE] and others tell you how to take your programming to the extreme, in part by using test-driven development.

Each of these luminaries describes an essential part of the use of testing in software development. Each of their works uses extensive examples to help you understand their particular teachings.

However, as I have coached teams into testing regimens, I have repeatedly found that the obstacle to adoption is neither a lack of understanding of the process flow, nor a misunderstanding of the concepts, nor an insufficient lexicon, nor skepticism about the value of the practices. All of these obstacles exist in various people at different times, but the most common one that has not been well addressed is simply limited understanding of the mechanics of testing code and of writing testable code.

While this book focuses on the mechanics—the implementation patterns—of programmatic testing and testability, you will apply the techniques more adroitly if you approach the book with an understanding of the conceptual framework that motivates it. Part I examines the relationship between engineering and craftsmanship and the role of testing in craftsmanship. It then shows you how to approach the testing of existing and unwritten code, how to better understand the intent of code, what testability looks like, and guiding principles to keep in mind as you write your tests.

Chapter 1

Engineering, Craftsmanship, and First-Time Quality

Our industry largely considers the titles software developer, computer programmer, code-slinger, and software engineer synonymous. However, in some places the latter title cannot be used because of strict regulation of the term "engineer." Software aspires to be an engineering discipline along with the more traditional engineering disciplines such as civil, mechanical, electrical, and aerospace. It has started to be recognized as such in recent years, but with considerable debate over questions of licensure, certification, and the minimal requisite body of knowledge.

At the same time, the software craftsmanship movement has grown steadily. With software craftsmanship groups around the world and events like CodeMash[1] and Global Day of Code Retreat,[2] an increasing number of developers want to focus on the skilled creation of code.

---

1. http://codemash.org
2. http://globalday.coderetreat.org

Engineering and Craftsmanship

One of the things that differentiates software engineering from other engineering disciplines is that we regularly and fully practice all aspects of the software construction process. Other types of engineers generally have interest and skills in their fields' associated construction processes, but they rarely live them as a daily activity.

Automotive engineers may spend time on the assembly line, but they do not work it regularly. Civil engineers may supervise and inspect the building of bridges or buildings, but they spend little time driving rivets, pouring concrete, or stringing suspension cables. Probably the closest to software engineers' total immersion might be the handful of test pilots who are also aeronautical engineers, in that they participate in design, construction, inspection, and verification of the craft they fly.

As a result of this renaissance approach to software, we tend to blur the lines between craft, engineering, and creative endeavor. Add to that a healthy dose of participation in the problem domain of our software, and it is no wonder that we entangle the concerns of our work. But what do I mean by that?

Professional software practitioners code, design, architect, test, measure, and analyze on multiple levels. Several of these activities clearly constitute engineering. The design and validation of others are also clearly engineering. But no matter how you cut it, the act of coding is an act of craftsmanship, of doing. We may "engineer" concurrently with the motions of our fingers on the keyboard, but we still exercise a craft.

The Role of Craftsmanship in First-Time Quality

Craftsmanship connotes skill. The skill with which we code affects the outcome of what we do. No matter how much we architect, design, or conceive our software, a poor implementation can undermine it all.

Traditionally, we relied on verification by our own attention or that of a quality assurance group to manually make sure the software behaved correctly. A developer once said to me, "I write my code, then I train it to do the right thing." While I lauded the underlying attentiveness to ultimate correctness, that statement also communicates a lack of intention for or attention to the initial product. The punch line came when he spent a week changing some core code in a complicated system and asked for three weeks to test the result.

Lean manufacturing operates under a principle of building the quality into a product. Rework is a form of waste to be eliminated from the system.[3] Writing software so you can rewrite it or patch it once the bugs are found is rework.

Testing software that should be correct can be seen as wasteful. Given that we have not figured out how to create software without defects, some degree of post-coding testing is required. However, testing it more than once is clearly inefficient, which is what happens when a defect is found, fixed, and retested.

Another form of waste is inventory, which can be seen as opportunity cost. Time spent fixing bugs is time during which the correctly written parts of the software have not been delivered and are therefore not delivering customer or business value. That time is also time in which a developer could have been working on other valuable activities, including professional development.

Improving the craftsmanship aspect of your work pays you and your company back with multipliers. It allows you to deliver more value with less waste in less time and with greater opportunity for personal satisfaction.

A Word on Methodologies

I will say up front that I am a fan of Agile and Lean approaches to software development. However, I am also a firm believer that there is no one methodology or family of methodologies that works best for every team, company, project, or product. I have done fairly standard software projects using both Agile and Waterfall approaches. I have done Agile development embedded in an otherwise Waterfall process. I have even applied largely Agile techniques to products that involved real-time control and human safety concerns. I have also taken very aggressively Agile and Lean approaches to cutting-edge web development with an aim toward full organizational transformation.

Regardless of the methodology you use, you probably have some form of automated testing in your project, if for no other reason than that you are tired of pressing the buttons yourself. More likely, you have some form of continuous integration system with unit, integration, system, component, functional, and other forms of test running frequently.

And where there is test automation, someone is writing code that tests other code. If that is the case, you will find the techniques in this book useful. For unit or isolation testing, almost all of the techniques will apply. For larger scopes of testing, you may have fewer options to apply. Some techniques will only pertain

---

3. There are many references on Lean, the Toyota Production System, and waste (or *muda*) in that context. An accessible place to start is http://en.wikipedia.org/wiki/Toyota_Production_System.

to some languages. You can use others in almost any language or programming paradigm.

I mention approaches to testing that are common in the Agile playbook. Do not let that deter you from trying them if that is not your flavor of development. Whether you practice test-driven development, test first, test early, or test after, you still need to tame the code under test. Happy testing!

Practices Supporting Software Craftsmanship

The question then becomes: How can we constantly increase the likelihood that our software is correct from the start? First, let computers do what computers do best, the rote mechanical activities and detailed analyses that are time-consuming and error-prone for humans. The ways we can leverage automated code quality tools leads to a taxonomy of software hygiene.[4]

- Style: Whitespace, curly braces, indentation, etc.
- Syntax: Compilation, static analysis
- Simplicity: Cyclomatic complexity, coupling, YAGNI[5]
- Solution: Runtime, correctness, whether it works, TDD, BDD
- Scaling the effort: Continuous integration, continuous delivery

Starting with the integrated development environment (IDE),[6] we have a wealth of features at our disposal covering Style to Solution. Code completion, syntax highlighting, and project and file organization and management only start the list. Refactoring support and other tool integrations sweeten the pot. If you can, configure all of your tools to give immediate, real-time feedback within your IDE. The less time that passes between when you write the code and when you get the feedback, the closer you come to first-time quality.

Do not concern yourself with the placement of curly braces and the amount and type of whitespace. Configure your IDE or your build to

---

4. Thanks to Zee Spencer for his suggestions in this area.

5. "You aren't going to need it" from extreme programming. [XPI, p. 190]

6. Or your editor of choice. A number of text editors, such as Sublime Text (www.sublimetext.com), support many IDE-style features in a lighter-weight package.

do all of your formatting for you. Ideally, your IDE will do it so that it is applied instantly. The next best thing gives that responsibility to a build target that you can run locally at any time.

Further protect yourself with static analysis tools to help with Syntax and Simplicity. Tools like Checkstyle for Java, jshint or jslint for JavaScript, perlcritic for Perl, lint for C and C++, or the equivalent for your language of choice help to check for stylistic problems. More sophisticated tools like PMD[7] or FindBugs for Java go beyond formatting and style and explicitly look for everything from unused and uninitialized variables to framework-specific conventions and complexity metrics. Some are even extensible. PMD in particular has a very flexible capability to define rules based on XPath expressions against the abstract syntax tree. PMD also has a module called CPD, the copy–paste detector, that highlights code that was copied when perhaps it should have been refactored to reuse.

Code coverage tools help you guide your testing by numerically and graphically showing you what parts of your code have been executed, guiding you toward the right Solution. We will look more closely at code coverage ahead.

Code generation tools will create thousands of lines of code based either on your source or their own domain-specific language, potentially helping with Simplicity and Solution. Tools exist to generate network service interfaces, database access code, and more, even though in many cases the use of code generation is a code smell[8] of a missed opportunity for code reuse, also Simplicity. In some cases, you even have tools to help generate your tests. If you trust your code generator, you can skip testing the generated code, saving time and effort on two fronts.

Finally for tools, continuous integration can run all of these tools along with the build and the tests to provide qualification of your code independent of the local environment, helping with Scaling. The results of the continuous integration builds should be available via the web, on monitors, and through e-mail. Many groups have tied their

---

7. PMD is a static analysis tool for Java and other languages. It can be found at http://pmd.sourceforge.net. The developers claim that it is not an acronym, but a "backronym." See http://pmd.sourceforge.net/meaning.html for explanation and possible interpretations.

8. Another of Kent Beck's contributions to software craftsmanship, meaning a symptom of deeper problems.

failing continuous integration results to sirens or flashers to make it obvious. Continuous integration builds should provide results in minutes for best effect. Continuous integration provides yet another form of rapid feedback, trading a little bit of responsiveness for a more comprehensive evaluation.

Testing

Of all the practices you can leverage to assist your craftsmanship, you will get the most benefit from testing. You may say, "We have been testing software for years, and we still have lots of bugs." Therein lies the key to going forward.

In a Lean system, you try to prevent defects rather than catch them. The tradition of software testing has been one of catching defects. It should not surprise us, then, that we have an inefficient process. The earlier you test, the sooner you catch defects.

Does that mean you are still just catching defects? If you write the tests after the code, then yes. If you close the gap between creating and catching the defects, less change occurs between the two events. You have a higher likelihood of the context of the created code being fresh in your mind. If you write the test immediately after writing the code, it can verify your conceptions and assumptions and keep you on course.

You also have an opportunity to really catch the bugs before they occur, however. Test-first and test-driven approaches to development bring the testing before the coding. When you test first, you capture your intent in an automatable and executable form. You focus on what you are about to write in a way that works to prevent defects rather than create them. The tests you write serve as a persistent reinforcement of that intent going forward. In addition to helping you do the *thing right*, it helps you to do the *right thing*. Remember, it is still a bug if you implement the wrong thing really well.

Within this model, **test-driven development** (**TDD**) is a subset of test-first approaches. Test first allows you to write as many and as fully coded tests as you want prior to writing your code. Test first brings the quality forward, but it gives you greater latitude to speculate about what you need and the form it will take. If you designed a solution that is more general than you need, you run the risk not only of spending more time in the creation, but also of creating a larger maintenance burden than you need, a cost that carries forward indefinitely. Additionally, writing too many tests in advance increases the cost of change if you discover a better approach to the problem. For these reasons, TDD gives you a more disciplined and leaner approach to the creation of software. You create just what you need right as you need it. The discoveries you make about insufficient foresight and incomplete prior understanding guide the direction of your code.

The principles put forth in this book will help you test effectively, regardless of when you test relative to when you code, but the earlier you test, the more this book will help. One of the guidelines around Agile development and testing is the Automated Testing Triangle (Figure 1-1). Traditionally, we have focused on system-level testing, which tends to either be brittle if it verifies too deeply or cursory if it aims to be more maintainable. We will never be able to replace system-level testing, but we can shift the balance of tests to lower-level unit tests.

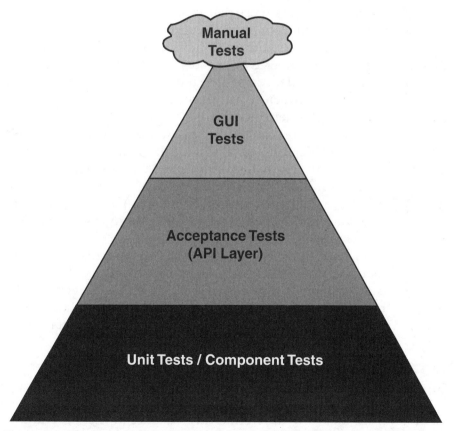

Figure 1-1: *The Automated Testing Triangle puts high investment in smaller tests because, when well written, they are less brittle and easier to maintain.*

I have heard people object to extensive unit tests on the grounds that they are brittle and hard to maintain. Well-written unit tests have exactly the opposite characteristics. The principles and techniques in this book will help you understand the reasons unit testing can become entangled and how to avoid them.

Unit Testing under Code Checker Constraints

Earlier, I mentioned that you should use tools to automate as many craftsmanship concerns as you can. If your tests drive the quality of your development, then you need to apply good craftsmanship to your tests as well. Not only should your tools check your application code, they should also check your test code to almost the same standards. I say "almost" because some reuse heuristics for production code need to be relaxed in test code. For example, repetition of string values between tests helps to keep your tests independent of each other, although using different strings is even better. Similarly, while refactoring for reuse benefits test code, you should not refactor tests in a way that blurs the distinction between setup, execution, and verification.

Applying static checker constraints to your unit tests will narrow the range of solutions you can apply. For example, a chain of default PMD rules, if left in effect, will push you to take many of your constant values outside of your test methods if you need to use them in nested classes. You can address this in a number of ways, but if it becomes too much of a burden with little value for your team, you may want to apply a subset of your normal rules to your test code, or even an equivalent but customized set.

Regardless, treat your test code to the same standards as your application code and it will treat you well far into the future. If the form of some of the examples in the book seem a little strangely implemented, try implementing them the way you think they should look with static checkers turned on, and you will probably understand why.

Unit Testing for Coverage

Code coverage tools provide wonderful assistance in writing, crafting, and maintaining your tests. They graphically show you which code you executed in your tests, letting you know if you hit the code you intended and which code you have not hit yet.

Code coverage by no means gives you an exhaustive understanding of how you have exercised your code. Many constructs branch to multiple code paths in ways that cannot be statically determined. Some of the most powerful features of our various languages—the features that give us the most useful abstractions—work in ways that are transparent to static analysis. While the coverage tool may show you what has been executed when you use these mechanisms, it has no way to know in advance how many permutations exist in order to compute the degree of coverage from execution.

Data-driven execution replaces chained conditionals with lookups, generally from an array or table. In Listing 1-1, the coverage tool will give an accurate assessment of statement coverage for this case, but it cannot tell you whether each of the conditions represented as the transition points in the table have been covered as it could if you implemented it with chained `if...else` statements. If the functions in the `rateComment` array were defined elsewhere and potentially reused, the coverage tool would miss even more.

Listing 1-1: *An example of data-driven execution in JavaScript demonstrating a blind spot of code coverage*

```javascript
function commentOnInterestRate(rate) {
  var rateComment = [
    [-10.0, function() { throw "I'm ruined!!!"; }],
    [0.0,
      function() { gripe("I hope this passes quickly."); }],
    [3.0, function() { mumble("Hope for low inflation."); }],
    [6.0, function() { state("I can live with this."); }],
    [10.0,
      function() { proclaim("Retirement, here I come."); }],
    [100.0, function() { throw "Jackpot!"; }]
  ];

  for (var index = 0; index < rateComment.length; index++) {
    var candidateComment = rateComment[index];
    if (rate < candidateComment[0]) {
      candidateComment[1]();
      break;
    }
  }
}
```

Dynamic dispatch provides another mechanism by which code execution defies static analysis. Take the following simple line of JavaScript.

```
someObject[method]();
```

The value of the variable `method` is not known until runtime, making it impossible in the general case for a coverage tool to determine the number of available paths. In JavaScript, the number of methods can change over the course of execution, so the even the known methods of the object cannot be used to inform a coverage calculation. This problem is not restricted to dynamic languages. Even canonically statically typed languages such as C++, through virtual functions and pointer-to-member references, and Java, through reflection, have dynamic-dispatch features.

Other situations happen more naturally, what I call semantically handled edge cases. These are cases in which the language or runtime environment automatically translates exceptional conditions into variations that need to be handled differently from normal execution. Java unchecked exceptions, exceptions that do not have to be declared in the method signature, encapsulate a number of these, most famously the dreaded `NullPointerException` that occurs when trying to use a `null` reference. The handling of divide-by-zero errors across languages varies from full application crashes to catchable exceptions to the return of `NaN`[9] from the calculation.

Additionally, code coverage can deceive. Coverage only shows you the code that you executed, not the code you verified. *The usefulness of coverage is only as good as the tests that drive it*. Even well-intentioned developers can become complacent in the face of a coverage report. Here are some anecdotes of innocent mistakes from teams I have lead in the past that let you begin to imagine the abuse that can be intentionally wrought.

- A developer wrote the setup and execution phases of a test, then got distracted before going home for the weekend. Losing his context, he ran his build Monday morning and committed the code after verifying that he had achieved full coverage. Later inspection of the code revealed that he had committed tests that fully exercised the code under test but contained no assertions. The test achieved code coverage and passed, but the code contained bugs.

---

9. `NaN` is the symbolic representation of "not a number" from the IEEE floating-point specifications.

- A developer wrote a web controller that acted as the switchyard between pages in the application. Not knowing the destination page for a particular condition, this developer used the empty string as a placeholder and wrote a test that verified that the place-holder was returned as expected, giving passing tests with full coverage. Two months later, a user reported that the application returned to the home page under a certain obscure combination of conditions. Root cause analysis revealed that the empty string placeholder had never been replaced once the right page was defined. The empty string was concatenated to the domain and the context path for the application, redirecting to the home page.

- A developer who had recently discovered and fallen under the spell of mocks wrote a test. The developer inadvertently mocked the code under test, thus executing a passing test. Incidental use of the code under test from other tests resulted in some coverage of the code in question. This particular system did not have full coverage. Later inspection of tests while trying to meaningfully increase the coverage discovered the gaffe, and a test was written that executed the code under test instead of only the mock.

Code coverage is a guide, not a goal. Coverage helps you write the right tests to exercise the syntactic execution paths of your code. Your brain still needs to be engaged. Similarly, the quality of the tests you write depends on the skill and attention you apply to the task of writing them. Coverage has little power to detect accidentally or deliberately shoddy tests.

Notice that at this point I have not talked about which coverage metric to use. Almost everyone thinks of statement or line coverage. Statement coverage is your entry point, your table stakes, provided by almost all coverage tools. Unfortunately, many stop there, sometimes supplementing it with the even weaker class and method/ function coverage. I prefer minimally to use branch and condition coverage[10] as well. Several tools include branch coverage. Woefully few include condition coverage and beyond. Some additional metrics include loop coverage—each loop must be exercised zero, one,

---

10. Branch coverage evaluates whether each option in the syntactic flow control statements is covered. Condition coverage looks at whether the full effective truth table after short-circuit evaluation is exercised for complex conditions.

and many times—and data path metrics such as def-use chains[11] [LAS83, KOR85]. In Java, the open-source tool CodeCover (http:// codecover.org) and Atlassian's commercial tool Clover do well. Perl's Devel::Cover handles multiple metrics as well. Although its messages could use some improvement, PMD includes dataflow analysis errors and warnings for UR, DU, and DD anomalies.[12]

I seem to have an affinity for high-availability, high-reliability, and safety-critical software. I have led and worked on teams developing emergency-response software, real-time robotic control (sometimes in conjunction with non-eye-safe lasers), and high-utilization build and test systems for which downtime means real business delays and losses. I have led projects in which we treated 100% statement, branch, condition, and loop coverage as only a milestone to thorough *unit* testing. Not only did we only derive coverage from unit tests—as opposed to the many other levels of testing we applied to the systems—but we only counted coverage obtained for a class by the test for that class. Incidental coverage by use from other classes was not counted.

In general, I have found that you start to get a quality return at around 50% statement coverage. The return becomes meaningful as you approach 80%. You can get significant return as you pass the milestone of 100%, but the cost of doing so depends on your skill at testing and writing testable, low-complexity, loosely coupled code.[13] Whether the cost justifies your return depends on your problem domain, but most teams do not have the experience in achieving it to accurately assess the tradeoff.

---

11. Definition-use, define-use, or def-use chains are the paths from the definition of a variable to the uses of that variable without an intervening redefinition. See also http://en.wikipedia.org/wiki/Use-define_chain for the opposite analysis of a use of the variable and all the paths from definitions of that variable to the use without intervening redefinitions. The set of paths is the same for the two metrics, but the grouping is based on opposite end points. Coverage of these paths is a stricter form of coverage than is implemented in most tools.

12. See http://pmd.sourceforge.net/pmd-4.2.5/rules/controversial.html#Dataflow AnomalyAnalysis.

13. These milestones are purely anecdotal, but correlate well with the observations of others, including http://brett.maytom.net/2010/08/08/unrealistic-100-code-coverage-with-unit-tests/ and the common targets of 70–80% coverage in many organizations. There are several possible explanations for this effect, ranging from the fact of the tests to the increased focus on design from practices like TDD.

Typically, teams choose an arbitrary number less than 100% based on arguments that it is not worth it to reach 100%. Generally, arguments for what not to test fall into two groups: the trivial and the difficult. Arguments against writing the difficult tests focus on either the algorithmically complex items or the error paths.

The trivial includes things like simple getters and setters. Yes, they can be boring to test, but testing them takes little time and you will never need to wonder if your coverage gap is only due to the trivial omissions.

The algorithmically complex code is most likely the heart of your secret sauce—the thing that distinguishes your software from everyone else's. That sounds to me like something that requires testing. If the implementation complexity discourages testing, it probably needs design improvements, which can be driven by the need for testability.

The error path tests verify the parts most likely to upset your customers. You rarely see kudos in online reviews for software that does not crash and that handles errors gracefully. Software that crashes, loses data, and otherwise fails badly gets poor and very public reviews. In our eternal optimism, we developers hope and almost assume that the error paths will rarely be traversed, but the reality that the world is perfectly imperfect guarantees that they will. Testing the error paths invests in your customers' good will under adversity.

Ultimately, you make the decision about the degree of testing your business needs. I recommend that you make that decision from the position of the skilled craftsman who can achieve whatever coverage the business requires rather than from the position of avoiding high coverage because it seems too hard. The purpose of this book is to fill out your tool belt with the patterns, principles, and techniques to make that possible.

Chapter 2

Intent of Code

Have you ever found yourself working in your favorite IDE with all of its bells and whistles (syntax checking, auto-completion, static analysis, and other features) and lamented the lack of one particular feature that hasn't been invented yet? Yes, I'm referring to the Intention Checker. You know it. The feature you wanted when you thought, "I wish it would code what I meant and not what I typed!" Maybe you wanted it when you were struggling with a tricky algorithm. Perhaps you invoked it when you found that silly one-character bug. Whatever the circumstance, you've encountered the complexity of translating intention into implementation.

On the other side, we've all asked questions like "What is this code doing?" or the more extreme "What the @$!%& was this developer thinking?" Testing is all about verifying that the implementation matches the explicit or implicit intent of the development: explicit in that the code is supposed to accomplish some goal, implicit in that it is also supposed to do it with certain characteristics of usability, robustness, and so forth, regardless of whether they were specifically considered.[1]

---

1. It is important to consider that this occurs at many levels in the software development process. We translate what the user wants into what we think they want, what features we should add to address their need, how we map those features to our existing or desired application, how that fits into our architecture and design, and how we code it. Many of the points made in this chapter can extrapolate to the other levels.

Where Did I Put That Intent?

Intent can be a slippery thing. In broader society, you have phrases like "intentional living." When you practice intentional living, you attempt to treat every action as deliberate rather than habitual or accidental, with a consideration about the place and consequences of those actions in their context. Clarity of intention is also frequently associated with minimalist approaches. It takes more discipline and effort to practice it than is immediately obvious.

Software requires the same attentiveness. Having worked on a number of projects and products with human safety implications, I have become sensitive to the consequences of the code I write. These consequences extend to all software to some degree. The e-mail program that delivers mail to the wrong recipient can violate confidentiality and breach trust, sometimes with significant financial or political implications. The annoying crash of a word processor may seem trivial, particularly if no data is lost, but if you multiply it across millions of occurrences, it turns into a large quantity of irritation and lost productivity.

Minimalism also applies in software. The less code you write, the less you have to maintain. The less you maintain, the less you have to understand. The less you have to understand, the less chance of making a mistake. Less code leads to fewer bugs.

I deliberately include factors beyond safety, money, and productivity. Increasingly, software is integrated into everything and into devices that are with us much of our waking lives. This ubiquity gives software steadily increasing influence on the quality of our lives and our state of mind. Above, I included impacts like "trust" and "irritation." The intent of our products includes nonfunctional aspects. The companies with the greatest success capture not just the minds of their users, but also their hearts.[2]

Separating Intent from Implementation

An implementation is simply one way of many to accomplish an intent. If you have a clear understanding of the boundary between

---

2. If you really want to dive into this topic, consider *About Face* by Alan Cooper (Wiley, 1995) and its successors.

implementation and intent, you have a better mental model with which to write and test your software. Not infrequently, the implementation strongly resembles the intent. For example, an intent of "reward winning players" may implement as "query for winning users, iterate over them, and add a badge to each of their accomplishment lists." The implementation language closely corresponds to the statement of intent, *but it's not the same thing*.

Clearly delineating intent and implementation helps your testing efforts scale with your software. The more you can test the intent without incorporating elements of the implementation, the less you couple your tests to your code. Less coupling means that changes in implementation do not force you to update or rewrite your tests. Fewer changes to tests mean that less of your effort is spent on tests, and it increases the likelihood that the tests remain correct. All of this results in lower costs to verify, maintain, and extend your software, especially over the long term.

You can also separate the intent of your code from the function of your code. The distinction here divides the way the code was meant to work from the way it actually behaves. When you need to test implementation, you should test what the code is supposed to do. Testing that it behaves the way it was written provides a false sense of security if it was not written correctly. A passing test tells you something about the quality of the code and its fitness for purpose. A test that passes when it should not lies about those attributes.

When writing your code, use the features of your languages and frameworks to most clearly express your intent. Declaring a variable `final` or `private` in Java, `const` in C++, `my` in Perl, or `var` in JavaScript says something about the intended usage of the variable. In dynamic languages with weak parameter requirements such as Perl and JavaScript, passing hashes [PBP] or objects [JTGP], respectively, that name the parameter values can serve to document the intention more clearly internally.

A Simple Example That Makes You Think

Let's look at an example in Java. Listing 2-1 shows a simple Java class with several clues about its intent in the way it is constructed. Consider the `ScoreWatcher` class that is part of a system to track sports scores. It encapsulates the function of obtaining the scores from a news feed.

Listing 2-1: *A simple Java class to demonstrate intentional construction*

```java
class ScoreWatcher {
  private final NewsFeed feed;
  private int pollFrequency; // Seconds
  public ScoreWatcher(NewsFeed feed, int pollFrequency) {
    this.feed = feed;
    this.pollFrequency = pollFrequency;
  }
  public void setPollFrequency(int pollFrequency) {
    this.pollFrequency = pollFrequency;
  }
  public int getPollFrequency() {
    return pollFrequency;
  }
  public NewsFeed getFeed() {
    return feed;
  }
  ...
}
```

First, look at the attributes defined for the class. The class author defined the `feed` attribute as `final`[3] while `pollFrequency` is not. What does this tell us? It expresses the intent that `feed` should only be set once on construction, but `pollFrequency` can be modified throughout the life of the object. The presence of both a getter and setter for `pollFrequency` but only a getter for `feed` reinforces that reading.

But that only gives us an understanding of the implementation intent. What functional intent might this support? We could make a reasonable conclusion in the context that exactly one of these classes should be allocated for each news feed we could use. We could also infer that perhaps there is exactly one `NewsFeed` per score to be monitored, which is used to initialize the `ScoreWatcher`. We could also speculate that the management of multiple feeds, if available, might hide behind the single feed interface. This would require verification but seems reasonable under the circumstances.

However, that hypothesis has a weakness that is probably due to a limit in the expressiveness of Java. Without knowing the construction of the `NewsFeed` class, we can speculate that it is possible to modify

---

3. In Java, the `final` keyword indicates that the declared variable cannot be changed once it has been initialized.

the object referenced by `feed` even though the reference itself cannot be changed. In C++, we could declare the attribute as

```
const NewsFeed * const feed;
```

which communicates not only that the pointer cannot be changed, but that you cannot use the pointer to change the object it references. This provides an additional marker of contextual immutability in C++ that does not exist in Java. It is relatively easy in Java to make all instances of a class immutable. It takes considerably more effort to make an object immutable through a particular reference, perhaps requiring the creation of an immutability proxy to wrap the instance.

So how does this change our tests? The construction of the class—the implementation—clearly specifies that the feed given to the class should not change during the lifetime of the class. Is this the intent? Let's look at a test that verifies that assumption in Listing 2-2.

Listing 2-2: *A test that verifies that the news feed does not change in Listing 2-1*

```
class TestScoreWatcher {
  @Test
  public void testScoreWatcher_SameFeed() {
    // Set up
    NewsFeed expectedFeed = new NewsFeed();
    int expectedPollFrequency = 70;

    // Execute SUT⁴
    ScoreWatcher sut = new ScoreWatcher(expectedFeed,
      expectedPollFrequency);

    // Verify results
    Assert.assertNotNull(sut); // Guard assertion
    Assert.assertSame(expectedFeed, sut.getFeed());

    // Garbage collected tear down
  }
}
```

In JUnit, the `assertSame` assertion verifies that the expected and actual references refer to the same object. Going back to our speculation about the intent of the class, it is reasonable to assume that it is important to reference the same feed, but is the same `NewsFeed` an overspecification of that condition? For example, what if the

---

4. SUT is an acronym for Software Under Test. [xTP]

implementation chose to enforce the immutability of the initial news feed by cloning the attribute before returning it from the getter, thus ensuring that any changes did not affect the internal state of the `ScoreWatcher`'s `NewsFeed`? In such a case, testing for the identity of the constructor argument is incorrect. The design intent more likely requires verifying the deep equality of the `feed`.

Chapter 3

Where Do I Start?

Knowing how to approach a problem and having a plan of attack simplifies and increases the effectiveness of testing. In this sense, test-driven development provides an easier framework in which to test because your tests are directed by what you want to implement next. Untested existing code presents a more formidable challenge because there are so many options for how to start.

This chapter provides guidance in the form of a reasoned approach to testing. The strategy is not radical or new, but it establishes a context in which the techniques in the remainder of the book can be applied. It hopefully clears away some of the questions about testing strategy so that testing techniques can be used effectively.

This chapter—in fact, this whole book—focuses on automated testing. In the Agile Testing Quadrants identified by Lisa Crispin and Janet Gregory [AT], it is all about Q1 and Q2, the quadrants that support the team.

An Approach to Testing

No one has discovered the magic formula for perfect testing. This means that, as practitioners, we need to apply a combination of reasoning, experience, and intuition when we write tests. This section captures many of the concerns you need to consider when writing automated tests.

Understand Your Scope

The first question you need to ask yourself is, "What am I trying to test?" This broad question includes the need to answer several more detailed questions, such as the following.

- Which use cases am I trying to verify?
- Are you trying to test the full stack, an integrated subset, or a unit?
- What technologies are you trying to verify?
- What architectural layers are you trying to verify?
- Are you testing new code, clean, well-written code, or are you rescuing a legacy hair ball?
- Can you decompose the testing problem into usefully smaller, more tractable pieces?

A full stack test gives you the ultimate verification of the fully integrated system, but at a cost. Full stack tests often run slowly due to the presence of all of the component interactions, including network, database, and file system. Full stack tests often have difficulty distinguishing nuanced behaviors and can require complicated recipes to induce error conditions because of the larger number of conditions that you must manage to achieve those results. Finally, full stack tests may be fragile or difficult to implement because of user interface and timing interactions. The smaller the scope of the test you tackle, the less these factors will have significance.

The technologies and architectural layers will naturally relate to your scope, but will steer the testing tools you use and influence your options for test doubles.[1] The testing frameworks you use to test a web interface are different from those for a ReST service, which are different from those for a Java class. Targeting the business layer may give you substitution options for the database, whereas testing stored procedures or ORM mappings may not.

The maturity and cleanliness of the code will guide your approach significantly. If you are starting a new project, you have the power to create the future. An existing exemplary code base makes your life easy, perhaps even boring, as you focus on the task at hand instead of reverse engineering and debugging. An unfamiliar spaghetti mess

---

1. Meszaros suggests the term "test double" as the blanket to cover the variety of stubs, fakes, mocks, etc. that can be used to support tests [xTP].

requires patience, insight, and a host of techniques from Michael Feathers [WEwLC]—such as characterization testing and seam[2] identification—before you can even start cleaning it up and adding features to it with confidence.

The more independent the parts of your system, the more likely you will feel confident testing those parts separately. Just like system decomposition, breaking your testing task into multiple subtasks will simplify your work and reduce your overall coupling.

A Conceptual Framework for Testing

For conceptual guidance, I use two principles to guide the overall shape of my testing efforts. First and foremost, I focus on the purpose of the software I am testing. Second, I actively work to reduce the degree of coupling introduced by the tests. Let's consider purpose now; we will discuss coupling in the next chapter.

The purpose of code applies differently at different levels. At a system level, the purpose of the code is the reason the software exists: its features, requirements, and use cases. Critical evaluation of the purpose helps to constrain your test cases and acceptance criteria. Is it important that a user interface element is a particular color or size or that it is aligned a particular way? You may not need to verify particular database fields if the value of the application is simply that the data or state is persisted and can be retrieved; exercising the retrieval and verifying the results may be sufficient.

At a module or component level, purpose refers to a function in the overall system. Integration tests satisfy the needs at this level. A module may overtly implement a feature, directly bearing the responsibility for the functionality the users expect. Alternatively, a module may implement an underlying, enabling design component. Either way, the module serves a role in the overall system. That role should be clear, and it needs to be tested.

At a unit- or isolation-test level, I like to think of the purpose as the **value added** by the code. Those who live in countries like Mexico or the European Union with a value-added tax (VAT) may find this concept clear. A company only pays a VAT on the amount of value it adds

---

2. The term *seam* is strongly intuitive, but to be precise, Michael Feathers defines a seam as "a place where you can alter behavior in your program without editing in that place" (p. 31).

to a product. Raw materials or component parts have a value when you receive them that is subtracted out of the value of the product you sell for purpose of taxation. Similarly, your code takes the libraries and collaborators on which it is built and adds an additional level of functionality or purpose for its consumers: the value added by that code.

Defining a unit test has caused considerable debate, but the value-added perspective gives us an alternative. Many have used definitions like that put forth by Michael Feathers[3] stating what a unit test does not do. I feel this merely codifies some test-design heuristics as rules and prefer to use the value-added concept for an inclusive definition of a unit test.

> A unit test is a test that verifies the value added by the code under test. Any use of independently testable collaborators is simply a matter of convenience.

With this definition, use of an untestable method in the same class falls within the value added by the code under test. A testable method called from the code under test should have independent tests and therefore need not be part of the verification except to the extent that it adds value to the code under test. Use of other classes can be mocked, stubbed, or otherwise test doubled because they are independently testable. You can use databases, networks, or file systems at the expense of test performance, although I would not recommend it.

Every subset of the system, from the smallest method to the entire system itself, should have a well-defined purpose. If you find yourself struggling to test the subset, you may not know its purpose. If you do not know the purpose of the subset, it probably has some implementation, design, or architectural issues. You have just diagnosed current or future problems maintaining and extending your software simply by looking at it through a particular lens in order to test it.

State and Behavioral Testing

Classifying the testing task at hand aids in identifying the best approach in writing the tests. Determining whether a test will verify state or behavior usefully steers the testing process.

Pure state verification exercises the code and examines the resulting changes in data values associated with the operation. Mathematical

---

3. See his blog entry on the topic at www.artima.com/weblogs/viewpost .jsp?thread=126923. See also [WEwLC].

functions that simply transform inputs to outputs exemplify the target of state verification. In a functional model, verification simply determines that the return values correlate correctly with the input parameters. In an object-oriented model, you additionally verify that the attributes of the object have changed (or not changed!) appropriately. State verification tests typically supply inputs and verify that the outputs correspond to the inputs in the expected ways.

Behavior verification checks that the code under test performs the right operations: It exhibits the right behavior in ways that go beyond data transformation. The purest example of behavioral verification simply orchestrates activities, as in Listing 3-1. It is the method that only calls other methods that are independently testable in order to coordinate their execution order and to channel the outputs of one to the inputs of another. Behavioral testing relies heavily on test doubles, frequently mocks.

Listing 3-1: *A JavaScript example of a purely behavioral function using the* `jQuery.Deferred()` *implementation of the Promise pattern to coordinate asynchronous computation. It orchestrates the steps of the process, ensuring that dependencies are satisfied and parallel tasks are coordinated, but does no computation itself.*

```
function submitTestScore() {
  verifyAllQuestionsAnswered();
  $.when(
    computeScore(), // Returns deferred object
    allocateAttemptID() // Server call returns deferred object
  ).done(
    sendScore()
  );
}
```

Highly decomposed software tends to be either behavioral or stateful. You will encounter cases that justifiably do a little of both, but the majority of the software you test will fit cleanly into one category or the other, guiding you toward the most effective style for testing it.

To Test or Not to Test

Although most of this book assumes you want or need to test your software, you should not blindly assume that is necessary. Perhaps counterintuitively, the primary purpose of automated tests is not to verify new functionality. After you create the test, each time it runs it mainly serves to verify that you did not break existing functionality.

But what if you do not care about preserving functionality? If you write code that will be thrown away, consider whether you should write automated tests for it. Prototypes, proofs of concept, demos, and experiments may all have short and limited lives.

On the other hand, code that you want to sustain should be tested. If you test your code properly, you will increase your ability to modify your code safely. Code that you expect to base your business on and code that you want other people to use should be developed sustainably. This also means that the throwaway code just mentioned should be brought or rewritten under test if you decide to productize it.

You also need to decide how to test your code, and economics play a role in that decision. System and integration tests are usually cheaper and easier for highly coupled, low-quality code that changes infrequently. You will get more benefit applying unit tests to loosely coupled, high-quality code that changes often. The Automated Testing Pyramid presented in Chapter 1 assumes that you want to create sustainable software, but that may not always be the case for perfectly valid economic reasons. Or you may have inherited legacy code[4] that needs rescue, in which case you will wrap it in characterization tests [WEwLC]—essentially a form of system or integration test—until you can refactor it into the form more conducive to unit tests.

The Recipe

You can follow many different approaches to testing. You can test the rough functionality first and then selectively refine it. You can select a functional, architectural, or design section and dive into it thoroughly. There is value in taking a more ad hoc or random approach akin to manual exploratory testing. Yet another approach guides your testing by metrics, such as defect densities, complexity, or criticality.

This section details an approach, visualized in Figure 3-1, that I have found useful in driving toward high coverage, independent of how you select the code or functionality to test. The approach favors deep over broad testing. It works well when taking a test-driven approach to new code, but also applies well when reproducing bugs, enhancing existing code, or bringing existing code under test.

---

4. Michael Feathers [WEwLC] defines "legacy code" as any code without tests.

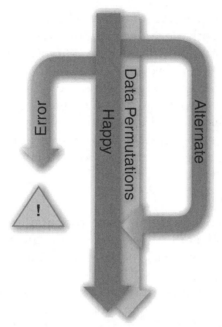

Figure 3-1: *Visualization of the testing recipe*

Test the "Happy Path"

The "happy path" of code or functionality is the primary purpose, the main reason the software exists. If you composed a single sentence to describe what the software does, you would describe the happy path.

Testing the happy path lays the foundation on which the rest of your tests are built. It establishes the context in which all of the variations add further value. In the sense of tests as documentation, it expresses the purpose in an executable form that can capture regressions and evolve with the functionality.

The happy path may require several tests to fully verify depending on the scope of the test. Start with the one or two characteristic purposes for the initial tests. For a unit test, a single test should capture it. For a full stack system test, it may require a suite of tests, but breaking that suite down into functional areas should make the task at hand manageable.

Test the Alternate Paths

Once you have established that the primary functionality works as intended, you can tackle the useful variations of normal behavior. For example, if the primary functionality was to save a file, special accommodations for network file systems might be a good alternate path. At a unit-test level, you might make sure that an event-processing loop functions properly when no events are queued.

At this point, your coverage targets should guide your thoroughness. If you are doing coverage-driven unit testing, then you will want to test exhaustively. You will most likely direct yourself by a sense of functional coverage for full stack system tests. Subsystem integration tests will strive for a more local definition of completeness.

Test the Error Paths

Many people stop before testing the error handling of their software. Unfortunately, much of the perception of software quality is forged not by whether the software fails, because it eventually will, but by how it handles those failures. The world is full of unexpected occurrences. Even if your software runs on stand-alone, hardened computers, it will eventually fail. Power fluctuations, magnetic interference, and component failure are just a few of the many things that can happen, often in a cascading chain.

Error-handling verification ensures that your response to the deviant variations in your environment are deliberate rather than accidental. Deliberate error handling should give your user the experience you desire and hopefully the one they desire as well.

Many organizations skip or skimp on error-path testing because of the difficulties involved. Generally, inducing errors in larger scopes is harder than in smaller ones. Simulating network errors at a class level is much easier than for a full stack application. Making error handling an architectural concern with clearly defined guidelines for how components should participate in that framework outlines the intent to verify at the lower levels, allowing you to focus on the correctness of the local behaviors.

Test the Data Permutations

Data[5] drives almost all software. When testing user interfaces and public APIs, boundary and validation conditions significantly impact the

---

5. I will talk only about the values used in testing here. Database testing warrants the attention of a whole different book.

security and stability of your software. At more programmatic levels, various forms of data-controlled behaviors can comprise non-trivial portions of the functionality. Even in statically typed languages like Java and C#, higher levels of abstraction in your system design naturally decrease the effectiveness of code coverage as a guide for complete testing. Dynamic languages and features like reflection-based execution compound the challenge.

Boundary Conditions

One of the more common forms of data variations in software behavior arises from boundary conditions. Boundary conditions occur for a wide range of reasons. Your happy and alternate path tests verify the behavior within normal input values, but may not test all input values. Boundary condition tests verify how the software behaves

- At the edges of the normal inputs to detect problems like off-by-one errors
- At the edges of the abnormal inputs also to detect off-by-one errors
- Using anticipated variations of abnormal inputs for concerns like security
- Using specifically dysfunctional abnormal inputs such as divide-by-zero errors or using inputs that trigger contextually determined limits such as numerical accuracy or representation ranges

You may have tested some boundary conditions when testing error paths. However, looking at the variations from the perspective of boundary conditions can highlight omissions in error-handling logic and drive more thorough test coverage.

Natural or pragmatic value and resource constraints provide a rich vein of boundary conditions. Natural limits occur when using values with a naturally finite set of states. True/false and yes/no are the most trivial of these. Menu picks that ask the user to choose from a limited number of options also provide contextually natural constraints. Pragmatic limits like field lengths yield a rich source of boundary conditions, especially when you manipulate or append to the input data internal to the software. At the resource-constrained or extreme end of the spectrum, you can test limits like memory and file size.

Numerical and mathematical variations can be thought of as natural or pragmatic but have a broad yet specialized enough affinity to deserve their own treatment and attention. Division-by-zero errors are perhaps the most common mathematical issues in programming, requiring attention regardless of representation format or size. Value limits due to discrete representations continue to factor into consideration, as the migration to wider representations is balanced by the inevitable increase in data volumes. Precision presents a more complicated set of conditions to test, as accuracy issues affect both the code being tested and the test code.

Standards- and convention-based formats yield structured and predictable, yet sometimes complex, patterns from which to derive boundary conditions, particularly as they evolve. For example, the syntactic rules of the Domain Name System (DNS)[6] are relatively simple. However, you can find opportunities for startling variations even within this simplicity. Security concerns drive people to attempt to validate domains. Those who choose not to validate them through lookup, regardless of whether for good or bad reasons, must make assumptions about the rules of domain names that go beyond the syntactic conventions. I have seen code that assumes that all top-level domains (TLDs) must be two or three characters in length, as was true for most of the original set of TLDs. This ignores the originally allocated single-letter domains used for administrative purposes and does not automatically account for the longer TLDs that have been and will be added, such as .name and .info. Expansion of the DNS syntax to allow non-European character sets adds another wrinkle to validation.

More ad hoc or unstructured sources provide some of the most challenging inputs to predict. Any free-form text field has numerous considerations to validate. The simplest may involve restrictions on or stripping of white space or selection from a limited character set. The more complex can include evaluating inputs to detect SQL injection or cross-site scripting attacks and natural language processing for semantic content.

Data-Driven Execution

Guiding tests by code coverage, particularly at the unit level, works well to test behavioral variations that derive from code structure. However, many constructs provide significant behavioral variations without explicit branches in the code. The so-called Fundamental

---

6. See http://tools.ietf.org/html/rfc1035#section-2.3.1.

Theorem of Software Engineering[7] says, "We can solve any problem by introducing an extra level of indirection."

A common data-driven scenario arises when processing command-line or some remote-invocation interfaces in which a dispatcher uses an Abstract Factory to generate Command pattern [DP] objects for execution, as shown in Listing 3-2. The function of the `CommandFactory` and each of the available `Command` implementations should be tested in their own right, but the `CommandDispatcher` integrates the behaviors to create a larger set of behaviors that cannot be identified through static analysis or evaluated for coverage.

Listing 3-2: *A dispatcher using an Abstract Factory in a data-driven way to create Command pattern objects to do the work*

```
class CommandDispatcher {
  private CommandFactory commandFactory;

  public void dispatch(String commandName) {
    Command command =
      commandFactory.createCommand(commandName);
    command.execute();
  }
}
```

When testing these constructs at the unit level, we should verify the correctness of the dispatch mechanism. Ideally, the definition of the dispatch targets is dynamic or separate in a manner conducive to independent testing. We should test each of the dispatch targets independently.

For tests at a larger scope, like system or integration tests, we must test each of the dynamic variations to ensure thorough testing of the software. A dispatch mechanism that works generically at the unit level typically has a well-defined and finite set of possibilities when integrated into a component or system.

Run-Time and Dynamic Binding

Most languages that run in a virtual machine and/or are dynamically bound like scripting languages have a feature called reflection. **Reflection** provides the ability to inspect the program's namespace at

---

7. Not really a theorem; there are conflicting attributions for this quote. See http://en.wikipedia.org/wiki/Fundamental_theorem_of_software_engineering and http://en.wikipedia.org/wiki/David_Wheeler_%28computer_scientist%29 for two of them.

runtime to discover or verify the existence of elements like classes, functions, methods, variables, attributes, return types, and parameters and, where applicable, invoke them.

The ability to access or invoke arbitrary symbols resembles a built-in form of data-driven execution based on data maintained by the runtime system but with a higher degree of capability and flexibility than most applications will create on their own. The power of reflection has led many teams to discourage or outright ban it from their applications to avoid some justifiably distasteful uses. In languages like Java (Listing 3-3) or Perl, this will not inhibit most applications excessively. Languages like Smalltalk and JavaScript (Listing 3-4) suffer without the use of these features. Even if your team avoids writing reflection-based code, many frameworks, like Java Spring and Quartz, use reflection extensively to enable configuration-based application assembly and dependency injection.

Listing 3-3: *Basic dynamic invocation in Java using reflection, omitting error handling and exceptions*

```
class Invoker {
  public static void invokeVoidMethodNoArgs(String className,
      String methodName) {
    Class clazz = Class.forName(className);
    Object object = clazz.newInstance();
    Method method = class.getMethod(methodName, null);
    method.invoke(object, null);
  }
}
```

Listing 3-4: *Basic dynamic invocation in JavaScript*

```
function invokeNoArgsNoReturn(object, func) {
  if (object[func] && typeof object[func] === "function") {
    object[func]();
  }
}
```

Even less capable languages for reflection, such as C and C++, can exhibit some of the dynamic-binding properties of reflection-able language through POSIX dynamic library APIs like dlopen(3) as shown in Listing 3-5. This API gives the application the ability to load a shared library dynamically and to invoke functions within it, all by specifying the library and function names as strings under the constraint that the invocation signature is known.

Listing 3-5: *Runtime binding with the POSIX dynamic library API in C without error handling*

```c
#include <dlfcn.h>

int main(int argc, char **argv)
{
  void *lib;
  void (*func)(void);
  lib = dlopen(argv[0], RTLD_LAZY);
  func = dlsym(lib, argv[1]);
  (*func)();
  dlclose(lib);
  return 0;
}
```

Just as in data-driven execution, tests need to verify that the mechanism for the dynamic invocation works at the unit level and that the assembled pieces work together at the higher levels.

Test the Defects

No matter how much you test your code, there will be defects. If your team does its job well, you will find all of your significant defects before you get to production. Regardless of when and by whom the defect is found, writing a test that duplicates the defect and then passes after the fix helps you know that you have fixed the defect and ensures that the defect remains fixed over time.

I prefer to test each defect, at least at the unit level. Every defect, including defects that can be broadly described as integration or interaction problems, trace to one or more defects in a unit of code. Perhaps the caller passes the wrong parameters or invokes functionality in the wrong order. Perhaps the callee does the wrong thing with the arguments or returns the wrong format or value. Maybe the synchronization is handled in a way that allows occasional race conditions. All of these and more can be duplicated and fixed at the unit level.

Chapter 4

Design and Testability

Much has been written about software design. Our body of knowledge and vocabulary about design concerns have continually evolved over the last several decades. We have applied structured design, object-oriented design, and aspect-oriented design to our software. We speak of design patterns and pattern languages as catalogues and guiding principles. Meszaros [xTP] compiles patterns about the testing of software.

In all of this, very little has been said about designing our software to be testable. Testability often comes as an afterthought or we sacrifice testing for the purity of our design. In fact, many of our "good design" principles inhibit testability. This chapter will examine some ways in which this occurs.

A Word on Design Paradigms

I make many of the points in this chapter in the context of object-oriented (OO) design, which is the dominant design paradigm at the time of this writing and for the prior two decades. The issues I bring up here are not unique to OO. If anything, the variety of encapsulation mechanisms available in most OO languages give you a wider range of solutions to the problems I am highlighting. On the other hand, the number of mechanisms and the conventional wisdom that typically go with those mechanisms provide many ways to make code difficult to test or untestable.

As our industry matures, the general attitude toward testing is changing dramatically. The ready and continuingly increasing availability of computing power makes it an easy decision to run automated tests continuously. Lean-inspired approaches like extreme programming and practices like test-driven development push us to write our tests first to build quality in and to drive our designs. The ubiquity of software in our society increases the need to test software extensively and quickly.

However, our design paradigms and the programming languages that implement them have not kept up. We need to understand the limits of our design approaches in a world in which software is more important than ever before and software quality is a business decision. Whether you are working in a procedural, functional, or object-oriented frame, you need to consider testability as a design factor.

Encapsulation and Observability

Implementation hiding is a fundamental principle of object-oriented encapsulation. An object represents a thing as a whole. It may have characteristics or attributes, but the underlying data that represents them is not necessarily the same as the external representation. Similarly, we suppress subsets of class behaviors that do not directly manifest in the external representation, because they are one of many possible implementations or they do not make sense in isolation.

Representational Encapsulation

Data types do not tell the full story of the representation either. Although much of the discussion about object-oriented design is in the direction of structure and syntax—the mechanics of encapsulation—you can make a strong case that meaning is the most important aspect. The purpose of an object and its characteristics need to be at the forefront of your mind as you design and use them. Ideally, the object design guides you toward the correct usage, but mainstream programming languages currently have little provision to encode full semantic intent.

With respect to the usage of an object, all of this protects us from creating objects with inconsistent internal state and provides the object's implementation avenues for enhancement that preserve compatibility. Using methods to control access to attribute implementations hides any complexities in managing the internal state. It also allows the internal representation to change without requiring changes on the part of the users of the interface, when done properly.

However, this same level of indirection interferes with the verification of our implementation. Only the rare and simple object requires nothing more than its specification to be thoroughly tested. Driving testing by coverage further ensures a need for deeper visibility.

Consider the example of an object that buffers I/O, similar to Java's `BufferedReader`[1] class. The class should not expose the internals of buffering because the typical user only wants to read a stream more efficiently. Noticing that `BufferedReader` only implements the `Closeable` and `Readable` interfaces further underscores that intent.

The implementer of a buffered I/O class cares tremendously about the internal behavior of the object. Reading characters into the buffer, the number of characters in the buffer, and how the system behaves when the buffer is drained or when full all support the correctness of the functionality. Tightly encapsulating the implementation leaves the object hard to test. The developer can relax the strictness of the encapsulation in order to make it more testable and document that the exposed entry points should not be used, but users of the class can—and likely will—ignore the warnings at some point in time. Various languages provide other mechanisms that can be used to access the internals of the class, as examined in Chapter 9, but most of these mechanisms amount to forcibly prying open the locked box.

Behavioral Encapsulation

A similar set of considerations occurs with methods and subordinate objects. As the implementation of an object's behavior grows, the size and complexity of its methods increase, leading to refactoring. This refactoring creates new methods and classes, some of which represent purely internal models of behavior within the object. The Extract Method [REF] refactoring creates restricted methods. The Extract Class

---

1. http://docs.oracle.com/javase/6/docs/api/java/io/BufferedReader.html

[REF] refactoring creates a new representation that may not need to be seen outside of the original context.

Refactoring like this tames the size and complexity of the software. However, the very size and complexity that suggests refactoring also suggests the need for testing. We may simplify a component or unit of our software by refactoring, but in the process we have also identified a critical step in a process or an actor in a relationship. The criticality of the new elements requires testing.

Many in the object-oriented development community say that you should not test private methods. This opinion certainly supports the strict encapsulation of the object. However, this position also holds a high chance of increasing the complexity and maintainability of our tests as we set up the conditions to invoke the extracted elements in all the necessary ways. The complexity incurred in the tests then becomes opportunity for errors in the tests, making our test cases less reliable. Direct testing of refactored implementations provides the same kind of simplification in our tests that refactoring produced in our production code.

Shades of Testing

Testing is a monochromatic but varied discipline. Black-, white-, and gray-box testing frequent the vocabulary. **Black-box testing** aims to test the software based on the exposed functionality and external contract. On the other hand, **white-box testing** verifies the software with full knowledge of the internals. Somewhere in the middle of the spectrum, **gray-box testing** has been represented as black-box testing with educated guesswork about the internals or as white box-testing constrained by the portions of the internal knowledge that could be reasonably inferred or expected.

A desire to minimize the coupling between our tests and our code motivates this graduated taxonomy. If we only test what is externally promised by our objects, we will not make unwarranted assumptions in writing our tests. Many people feel that we should only write black-box tests as we move increasingly from the finer granularity of unit tests out to the coarse granularity of system tests. We will see later in the chapter that black-box testing is not sufficient to avoid coupling our tests to our implementations and that a greater degree of coupling arises from standard object-oriented design guidelines than we usually realize.

Black-box testing cannot sufficiently test our implementations, as shown by the buffered I/O example earlier. That leaves us to supplement it with white- or gray-box tests for thorough functional coverage, regardless of whether we use code coverage targets. However, tests with internal visibility often require the same kind of internal access that encapsulation aims to prevent.

Dimensions of Testing

Several considerations intersect when talking about tests. For example, have you ever heard someone ask if a test is a unit test or a regression test? Are they really mutually exclusive? Let's examine the different dimensions encountered when talking about tests.

The first dimension is purpose. Why do I want to write or run this test? A regression test makes sure that the behavior has not changed (i.e., regressed) over time. When you practice test-driven development (TDD), the tests document the usage scenarios and guide the low-level design. A test's purpose can change over time. The test originally written for TDD becomes a regression test shortly into the initial TDD session. Acceptance tests verify that software meets its functional purpose from a user perspective; they verify that the software is ready to be accepted. Performance tests check that the system is sufficiently responsive with low latency and so forth. Smoke testing provides quick but cursory verification.

Granularity is another dimension. What is the scope or boundary of what you are trying to test? The term "unit" when speaking of unit tests refers to the idea that you are testing the smallest unit of code, such as a function, method, or class. Because of extensive debate on the definition of a unit test, some people prefer the term "isolation test" because it isolates a well-defined section of code. Larger granularities include integration tests that exercise combinations of units or components and system tests that verify the whole system.

Yet another dimension is transparency, as discussed in the Shades of Testing section. Black box only tests overt behaviors with no consideration of implementation. Gray box considers probable implementations and algorithmic gotchas. White box is guided by the implementation.

Another dimension describes the approach to testing. Monte Carlo testing, monkey testing, and random event testing each refer to techniques for "surprising" your code in ways that deterministic tests cannot.

Recognize the important dimensions when you talk about tests. Although certain points in a dimension may be frequently associated with points in another dimension—acceptance and performance tests are usually system tests, for example—we should not assume that the typical associations always apply. We should especially avoid transposing the associations or forgetting that they can change over time and with context.

Encapsulation, Observability, and Testability

All in all, conventional guidance about object-oriented encapsulation creates a tension between good design and testability. The testability of a class directly relates to your ability to verify its state, hidden behind getters and setters, and its behavior, hidden in restricted methods.

In an ideal world, our programming languages would support testability needs. Increasingly, frameworks make provisions for testability and tools leverage language features to increase our ability to test. In the meantime, our job is to find a balance between the rules of good design and the need for verification.

This book advocates using language and tool features where possible to test our code. Where standard language features are unavailable, we will examine the ways in which you might relax design constraints with the least violation of the spirit and purpose of encapsulation.

Coupling and Testability

Coupling is the degree to which one section of code depends on another. Clearly, test code depends on the code it tests based on the nature of that relationship. For black-box testing, test code depends on the interface of the test target as well as any data types or dependent interfaces or signatures used in the interface. If a method takes a type in its parameter list, the calling code—and therefore the tests—need to be able to obtain or create that type. When a method returns a type, the calling code uses that value, expressing a degree of knowledge about that type. The same holds true even when interfaces are used because interfaces specify types. Functional, procedural, and dynamic languages are not immune to this effect. The signatures—the return types and parameter lists—of callbacks, listeners, functors, etc. all introduce additional coupling to our code.

White- or gray-box tests may create additional dependencies as we test restricted methods that are not part of the public contract and as we test implementations that use types that are not otherwise exposed. It is not uncommon to have internal and entirely private abstractions that support the implementation.

All of these relationships between test code and the code under test increase the degree of coupling between the test and the test target. Thorough testing tends to maximize the potential coupling between the two participants.

Software design aims to minimize coupling. Coupling measures dependencies between components. Dependencies may represent a necessary use of provided functionality to achieve the business purpose of the software. However, the decomposition of software for any given problem into components is only one of many possible solutions. Often the initial implementation needs to change as the software grows and the functionality increases. If the interfaces were designed with enough foresight and luck, the component can be refactored, preserving the external behavior and contract for all callers. No such guarantee exists for gray- or white-box tests, as refactoring does not commit to preserve the implementation details. In more extreme cases, we must rewrite the component, likely breaking or invalidating all calling code, including the black-box tests.

The evolution of a software product forces changes in code, particularly in tests. Often people justify lower levels of testing based on this effect. That does not need to be the case. Neither the existence of tests nor the fact of code change causes tests to become brittle. Just as we design our software to be less brittle internally as it evolves, we can apply principles of design for testability to make our test code less brittle as well. This requires changing our concept of "good design" to extend to characteristics of testability as first-order drivers. Coupling is the enemy of scaling a testing practice, especially for unit testing.

Let's look at some aspects of this coupling in more detail. Ideally, a unit test couples to the unit under test[2] and only that unit. However, unless we constrain ourselves entirely to the fundamental data types of our language, that rarely happens in practice. Interfaces like the one from Java shown in Listing 4-1 or the one from JavaScript in Listing 4-2 often refer to other constructs in our most fundamental abstractions.

---

2. I will use the term "unit" in this section because the principles apply regardless of whether we are testing objects, components, modules, functions, or some other elemental building block, regardless of programming paradigm.

Listing 4-1: *A Java interface from the Swing package showing use of other classes. Note that the* `PropertyChangeListener` *comes from a package that is independent of Swing.*

```java
package javax.swing;

import java.beans.PropertyChangeListener;

public interface Action
    extends java.awt.event.ActionListener {
  java.lang.Object getValue(java.lang.String s);

  void putValue(java.lang.String s, java.lang.Object o);

  void setEnabled(boolean b);

  boolean isEnabled();

  void addPropertyChangeListener(
    PropertyChangeListener propertyChangeListener);

  void removePropertyChangeListener(
    PropertyChangeListener propertyChangeListener);
}
```

Listing 4-2: *A JavaScript functional interface from jQuery showing the use and representation subset of an event object. Even though JavaScript is dynamically typed, the convention of the contents of the event object couples callers to the signature.*

```javascript
jQuery.on( events [, selector] [, data],
    handler(eventObject) )

{
  target:
  relatedTarget:
  pageX:
  pageY:
  which:
  metaKey:
}
```

We overlook that the use of a type in an interface constitutes part of the contract of that interface. The use of the type can couple users of that interface to the additional type, increasing the overall coupling of the system. Because tests maximally use the features of the interface to get good code coverage, the tests use all of the parameter and return types. Typically, tests must create instances of parameters, invoking constructors, setters, and other methods, each coupling the test to those implementations and representations. Builders can abstract that coupling, but they introduce coupling to the builder. Test factory methods consolidate the dependencies, providing a shallow layer of insulation against coupling, but the coupling remains.

Similarly, tests use the return values from the methods in the interfaces to verify the results of operations. In the best cases, the tests can verify the return values through inherent equivalence (e.g., the Java `Object.equals()` method), a frequently hidden but relatively innocuous coupling. More often tests verify individual attributes or consequences driven by the need for partial comparison. Perhaps the effects of the aspect being tested do not require complete equality or there are less deterministic aspects of the class state (e.g., GUIDs or UIDs) that vary from instance to instance but relate to inherent equality nonetheless. Existing comparator objects and methods can minimize the coupling by substituting a lesser dependency in its place. Test-only comparators consolidate and mitigate the coupling as an improvement. But not all verification relies entirely on state, requiring use of the operations on these secondary types in the return interfaces.

One of the more common and insidious manifestations of these concepts occurs through the simplest of object-oriented conventions: attribute encapsulation. Typically, developers idiomatically write accessors for each of their attributes. The rationale is that it insulates the caller from the internal representation, allows for virtual or computed attributes, hides side effects, enforces immutability constraints, and so forth. Most commonly, though, the getter simply returns the internal representation, possibly providing direct access by reference to more complex internal structures. As we have seen, verification of those internal representations sometimes occurs through interface access. Where null safety is either guaranteed by the representation or ignored by the test, we see code like

```
A.getB().getC().getD()
```

Despite the blatant violation of the Principle of Least Knowledge,[3] we frequently find code like this—of course we do not write it ourselves!— in tests and production. Although the object states of A, B, and C are

---

3. Also known as the Law of Demeter, the Principle of Least Knowledge provides useful heuristics for minimizing coupling in software: http://en.wikipedia.org/wiki/Law_of_Demeter.

clearly encapsulated according to object-oriented standards, this construct of getter chaining transitively couples A to the implementations of B, C, and possibly D.[4]

All of this serves to exacerbate the tension between the principles of good design and the practical forces driving development. Normally, we might write off a translation between internal representations and interface representations as a pedantic performance drain. This chapter motivates us to consider how the future maintainability of our test regimen impacts those design decisions.

Fortunately, there are lightweight ways to address these concerns. Through refactoring, we can introduce them on an as-needed basis as we grow our code and tests. The point here is not that we should cripple our performance and magnify our code to thoroughly insulate our tests from coupling with more than their direct test target. Rather, we need to approach our design and implementation in a way that factors these considerations into the balance intentionally.

---

4. Note that this is distinctly different from call chaining in which each call returns a reference to the representation being acted on as is often implemented for compact setting of state with a functional flavor.

Chapter 5

Testing Principles

Although this book has many specific recipes for testing particular circumstances, several of the techniques may be applied in a wide variety of situations. As with any skill, proficiency comes from learning the mechanics and practicing them. Real expertise comes from understanding the reasons behind the mechanics. This chapter addresses that reasoning.

Applying these principles to your test writing will help you figure out which test patterns are relevant and which particular techniques to use. In the larger scheme, these principles will help you to scale your testing efforts to match the growth of your system without the disproportionate overhead that often occurs.

The principles are presented in order of importance. In general, I would give more weight to the earlier principles than the later ones when making decisions about testing approaches. That said, a solid and clear justification should beat a difference of a couple of places in the order. Ultimately, what is most important is well-reasoned design decisions, not rules.

Craft Your Tests Well

Your test code is almost as important as your production code. Treat it as such. This means you should craft it to nearly the same standards as your production code. In particular, you should

- Be sure to express the intent of your test in its code

- Try to express only the intent and nothing more to the greatest extent possible

- Keep your test code simple and clean, using the same tools with nearly the same configuration and refactoring as you go

In the interest of keeping it simple, I will not repeat all of the other tenets of well-crafted code. You will want to apply some principles of software craftsmanship slightly differently, however.

Some static checker rules should be disabled for test code. For one, most static checkers do not know that assertions throw exceptions, so they do not treat them as terminal statements in a function or method. You may also find it acceptable to let the runtime environment tell you values are `null` or `undefined` in some tests rather than asserting their validity at all places.

The structure of a Four-Phase Test [xTP]—setup, execute, verify, and tear down—should be preserved regardless of refactoring. If you are more familiar with the AAA structure—arrange, act, and assert[1]— then those are the boundaries to preserve. This means that you should not refactor across the phase boundaries. A little bit of repetition can better communicate the intent of the test.

A couple of other points deserve deeper treatment.

Couple Inputs to Outputs

How many times have you seen tests that resemble the following?

```
assertEquals(4, transformIt(2));
```

What are the meanings of the literal values 2 and 4 in this code? Sure, you can read the documentation, assuming it exists, for `trans-formIt()` and know what it is supposed to do. In the absence of documentation, you can look at the implementation and reverse engineer the code, but then you are testing implementation, not intent. Also, the author of code such as this requires each following developer to decipher his own intent in addition to whatever intent needs to be extracted from the code under test.

Would you rather see something like Listing 5-1 instead?

---

1. Originated by Bill Wake in 2001, also known as AAA or 3A. See http://xp123.com/articles/3a-arrange-act-assert/.

Listing 5-1: *Coupling inputs to outputs in tests*

```
int operand = 2;
int expectedSquare = operand * operand;

int actual = transformIt(operand);

assertEquals(expectedSquare, actual);
```

Although the example is a bit simplistic and contrived, the code reads in a much more intent-revealing way. Perhaps more importantly, the code clearly communicates the intended testing relationship between the input `operand` and the output `expectedSquare` to all future maintainers. If `transformIt()` changes, the test's prior expectation will be clear to all involved.

Use a Naming Convention

I almost omitted this. After all, everyone knows to use a naming convention, right? And everyone knows the benefits in terms of self-documenting code, maintainability, expression of intent, and so forth.

Then I remembered all the code bases I have seen with tests that have meaningless names such as `test1` and `test2`, incomplete conventions such as `testMethod` indicating that this is a test of `method` but not telling what aspect of the method is being tested, and inconsistent conventions. So here goes.

Use a convention. Use your convention consistently. Make sure your convention captures everything that needs to be captured. Seriously consider using industry-standard conventions, whether explicit or de facto standards, if they exist to minimize ramp-up time and retraining for new hires. If the convention needs to change, make sure you have a plan for how and when to change the instances of the old convention. Enforce your convention with static checkers where reasonable.

For tests, the elements of a good naming convention may include the following items.

- A syntactic marker to distinguish tests from nontests. Common examples include affixing the class with `Test`, prefixing test methods with `test`, and metadata markers such as JUnit and TestNG `@Test` annotations or NUnit `[Test]` attributes.

- References to the symbol under test such as using the class under test as the base name to which to affix `Test` and using the method under test as a component of the test method name.

- Description of the conditions or variations that distinguish the particular test such as meaningful values or business-rule contexts.
- Delimiters to separate the various components of the names.
- Guidelines on how to apply the convention for specific nonobvious cases. For example, should the test for the constructor of class `Class` start with `testClass` or `testConstructor`?

My particular current convention for tests (see Listing 5-2) in Java using JUnit or TestNG follows.

- Suffix the class under test with `Test` for forming the test class name. I use it as a suffix because a) it is the more common convention, b) I am working with lots of code that is about testing systems and naturally starts with `Test` already, and c) it avoids confusion with the tests for other suffixing rules, such as those for exceptions.
- Prefix test methods with `test`. It is a bit of a holdover from prior to JUnit 4, but I like how it clearly delineates test from nontest methods independent of the annotations.
- Use the method under test as the base name for test methods.
- Use "_" as a separator between the base test name and the description of the test variant, if a description is included.
- Add a brief description of the test variant. The description can be omitted for unique and obvious "happy path" cases.
- Constructor tests use the name of the class.
- Attribute getter and setter pairs are tested together with a method name starting with `testSetGet`.

Listing 5-2: *A brief demonstration of my current Java test-naming conventions in action. Note that the formatting is compressed for brevity.*

```
class Payment {
  public Payment(Double amount) { ... }
  public void setAmount(Double amount) { ... }
  public Double getAmount() { ... }
  public PaymentTransmissionResult transmit() { ... }
}

class PaymentTest {
  @Test public void testPayment () { ... }
  @Test public void testPayment_ZeroAmount() { ... }
```

```
  @Test public void testSetGetAmount() { ... }
  @Test public void testTransmit(){ ... }
}
```

Avoid Test Code in Production

Have you ever seen code like that in Listing 5-3?

Listing 5-3: *Example of test code in production*

```
public class MyClass {
  private boolean testing = false;
  public void doSomething() {
    if (testing) {
      // Mock something up
    } else {
      // Run the real code
    }
  }
}
```

I'm sure you have. Unfortunately, something like this or one of its variations exists in most code bases. Let's go over all the things that are wrong with this from a software-verification point of view.

First, how is `testing` set? I may have omitted a setter that would allow directly controlling the behavior through the interface. That would probably be the safest way to manage it. I've also seen people use a toggle interface instead. That is a little less safe because you have to always check the value to use it correctly. Both approaches are sometimes implemented without the corresponding getter. Maybe it is controlled through some form of dependency injection, in which case the value is separated from the implementation and the apparent default value may not be the truth. Another approach is to simply change the initialization in the code itself. But then what happens if the developer forgets to change it back before committing? If the mock is good enough, no one may notice until bad things happen after deployment to production. Each of these possibilities carries the risk that the test code can be turned on in production.

Next, ask yourself whether we can test all of the code. We cannot. If we turn on the testing flag, which we ostensibly want to do when we are testing, then we only run the first branch of the `if` statement. The second branch is only executed when we are not testing. That means that any code in the `else` branch will not be tested prior to deployment, introducing the risk of undetected bugs.

Finally, if you are using code coverage to drive your testing, this technique creates a "dark patch," a block of code that is uncoverable. This may be acceptable if you do not have code coverage targets or if your coverage targets have enough slack to absorb the amount of code in the `else` branch. Most of the code I have seen handled this way is critical initialization or resource-management code that significantly contributes to the behavior of the system. In addition to the untested aspect of the block, these kinds of holes in coverage lead to an expectation of incomplete coverage that weakens the value of coverage as a guiding metric.

Each of these risks compounds the more this technique is used. The chances of any one of the risks manifesting may be small, but each use of this technique increases the overall risk. If they are used broadly in a large enough code base, it is almost guaranteed.

The underlying principle is that test code should be kept separate from the code it is testing. Testing hooks should not intrude into the code under test in ways that are blatantly for testing. Design accommodations for testability should retain the integrity of the design and should preserve the intent of the code as much as possible.

Verify Intent over Implementation

As discussed in Chapter 3, all software has intent, and the first goal of testing is to verify the intent. Black-box testing is popular and effective because it verifies software purely by its intent rather than its implementation. However, most moderately complex algorithms or logic cannot be completely tested purely as a black box. Coverage-guided unit testing requires white-box insight into the implementation.

Notice that this principle says "intent *over* implementation" rather than "intent *instead of* implementation" as you find in more prescriptive statements. It is advisable and necessary to guide some level of testing, particularly unit tests, against the implementation, but you should never lose sight of the intent that the code is trying to produce.

Minimize Coupling

One of the primary arguments against extensive testing is that the maintenance of the tests creates an overhead that grows faster than the size of the source base. Most commonly, you will hear statements such as, "It's too hard to maintain all those tests."

In my experience, this effect can be almost eliminated by controlling the coupling[2] of the tests. The means to control the coupling varies depending on the type of test under discussion.

Coupling in system and integration tests generally occurs when the tests incorporate knowledge of the implementation in a white- or graybox fashion. Sometimes overzealous testers reach beyond the necessary behavioral guarantees of the system, but often coupling is a symptom of software that was not built for testability by not providing access to verify all effects of an operation.

For unit testing, coupling often takes more insidious forms. For example, object-oriented design principles suggest that all attributes should be encapsulated in getters and setters. While this encapsulation has several benefits, including the implementation of logical and lazy-loading attributes, it is a very thin encapsulation in the majority of cases, in which it wraps a value or reference. The return of a reference to a complex internal attribute is often an implementation detail of convenience rather than a requirement of the interface. When this happens, the interface of the class under test is coupled to the definition of the internally referenced object. The unit test in turn exercises the interface, resulting in transitive coupling between the test and the internal object.

These transitive coupling relationships resemble the increase in communication relationships as the number of people on a team increases. If each person in a team of n people communicates directly with one another, the result is $(n^2 - n)/2$ lines of communication. For four people, there are only six lines of communication, a relatively manageable number. For ten people, the resulting 45 lines of communication introduce inefficiencies. Twenty people have 240 lines of communication, an already unmanageable number.

---

2. The concept of *coupling* was introduced into the computer science lexicon by Edward Yourdon and Larry Constantine as part of structured design [SD]. It describes the degree of dependency between modules in a software system.

The techniques of this book are almost all focused in one way or another on reducing the coupling[3] between your test and its corresponding implementation. By reducing the coupling between your components, you reduce the coupling in your tests. Applying this principle results in much more scalable testing efforts.

Prefer Minimal, Fresh, Transient Fixtures

In *xUnit Test Patterns*, Meszaros [xTP] established a vocabulary for talking about tests. In particular, his terminology around fixtures clarifies and isolates a number of separable issues. This principle significantly leverages his terminology.

Fixtures establish the context for your test. They are the setup necessary to run your test. They construct, mock, dummy, inject, etc. the components necessary to run your test in as fast and isolated a way as possible.

Minimal fixtures are as large as necessary and no larger. Every fixture by necessity has elements that couple it to implementation. Although it is great to test by contract, you are testing real software with real implementation decisions. The more a fixture isolates the component under test, the more it behaves like other parts of the system. This couples it to those other parts, transitively coupling your test. In addition to making your tests faster and simpler, keeping your fixtures minimal reduces the coupling between your tests and the rest of the system.

Tests that use **fresh fixtures** recreate their fixtures for every test. The fresher the fixture, the less likely your tests will interact and the easier it will be to maintain each test in isolation from the others, reducing the coupling between tests.

Transient fixtures only exist for the duration of the test. They also act to reduce the potential interactions and coupling between tests.

The combination of minimal, fresh, and transient fixtures helps to reduce the coupling in your tests and to scale your testing effort in addition to providing the benefits of speed and isolation.

---

3. Coupling can be measured. See http://en.wikipedia.org/wiki/Coupling_%28computer_programming%29#Module_coupling for one approach.

Use Available Facilities

This is frequently expressed as "test through the interface." In the general sense, the statements are equivalent, but object-oriented programming languages have also given us a narrower interpretation that is not sufficient. This principle is broader than simply using the methods declared in an `interface`.

When writing tests, we want to minimize the degree to which we change the code under test to accommodate testability. The best way to do that is to use the features that already exist. This may be obvious for constructors, setters, and getters and completely natural and necessary for method arguments, return values, and other direct functionality. I have often seen other features of the code overlooked as potential hooks to support testability. Logging, monitoring instrumentation, factories, dependency injection, callbacks, and template methods all provide vectors through which to exercise greater control over the code under test. In the interest of containing complexity and preserving the intended design, existing facilities should be used before creating new ones.

Prefer Complete over Partial Verification

Many highly encapsulated systems hide internal state that they prefer not to let their client code manipulate. If such state is transient or implementation specific, that is probably the right decision. Sometimes developers hide these attributes as a matter of security instead. Security creates a compelling reason to hide, but should it be done at the expense of verification of relevant consequences? Getter-only access and cloned returns are two ways to provide visibility without weakening many security motivations, allowing more complete verification.

Another common category of incomplete verification is the use of substrings, collection membership, and other subsetting techniques to verify results. Containment is a relatively weak form of verification. Techniques for complete verification provide for much stronger tests. We will discuss these techniques in later chapters.

Write Small Tests

Small tests are easier to understand. Small tests are limited in their scope. Small tests most likely test one facet of the behavior. Small tests are less likely to incur coupling. Small tests are easier to diagnose when they fail. Need I say more?

Separate Your Concerns

Many of us think of separation of concerns when we design and code software but forget about it when we test. A common source of complexity in tests is a failure to separate the concerns.

For example, say you are creating a date-conversion library, two of the methods of which parse date strings into the underlying representation and format it into a display string. You could write a test that verifies the result by a round-trip, as in Listing 5-4.

Listing 5-4: *Testing date parsing and formatting through round-trip conversion in JavaScript with Jasmine*

```javascript
describe('DateLib', function() {
  it('converts the date back into itself', function() {
    var expectedDate = '17 Apr 2008 10:00 +1000';

    var actualDate = DateLib.format(
        DateLib.parse(expectedDate));

    expect(actualDate).toBe(expectedDate);
  });
});
```

However, you are actually testing two independent pieces of functionality: the parsing and the formatting. Just because you can test them together does not mean you should. Instead, test them separately as in Listing 5-5.

Listing 5-5: *Testing date parsing and formatting from Listing 5-4 as separate concerns*

```javascript
describe('DateLib', function() {
  it('parses a date properly', function() {
    var expectedTimestamp = 1208390400000;

    var actualDate = DateLib.parse('17 Apr 2008 10:00 +1000');
    expect(actualDate.getTime()).toBe(expectedTimestamp);
  });

  it('formats a timestamp properly for GMT', function() {
    var expectedDateString = 'Thu, 17 Apr 2008 00:00:00 GMT';
```

```
var inputDate = new DateLib.Date(1208390400000);

    expect(inputDate.toGMTString()).toBe(expectedDateString);
  });
});
```

By testing your functionality separately, you verify each operation independently and catch the case in which one bug compensates for another. You also more directly express the way in which each piece of functionality should be used.

Use Unique Values

The readability and usefulness of tests are enhanced when the values used to construct fixtures are mutually distinct. Within a test, unique values reinforce the differences between various assertions and help highlight when the implementation has miswired parameters or properties. Between iterations of a data-driven test, distinct values help to highlight the failing test case more clearly. The same effect applies between tests, in which case unique values also help to identify the effects of shared state.

Assertion failures generally provide good feedback on the values involved and the location in the code. However, some assertions, like `assertTrue`, do not display their contributing expression values. Assertions in loops will share a location for multiple data values. Custom assertions and assertions in fixtures or utility methods will show deeper stack traces than you would normally expect. In each of these cases, unique values help to localize the failure more quickly.

Data-driven tests magnify the shared location property of assertions in loops. The entire test is executed repeatedly rather than just the few lines in the loop. Unique values within a row help to distinguish the deviant property. Unique values within a column isolate the test cases regardless of which assertion fails.

Although best practice guides us away from tests that interact with each other, various shared resources ranging from static variables to singletons to files or databases can cause crossover, especially when tests are run in parallel. Unique values allow us to more easily notice when a value shows up in the wrong test or context.

Keep It Simple: Remove Code

You can simplify your tests and reduce your testing burden by deleting code. If the code does not exist, you neither have to test it nor have to maintain it. Remove unused code, commented code, code that does more than it needs to, and code that is more complex than it needs to be. Deleting code is a great way to reduce your costs.

Also, remove redundant tests. Even better, do not write them to begin with. Extra tests do not add to your validation, but they take time to run and attention to maintain. Just imagine how much time could be wasted trying to figure out what makes the redundant test different from the other tests in the same area.

If you use code coverage to guide your testing, removing code also increases your coverage. We usually think of increasing coverage by increasing the number of tests. But coverage is a percentage computed by dividing the number of features[4] exercised by the number of features that exist. We have two degrees of freedom to control the coverage, including reducing the total number of features. In the case of redundant tests, your coverage will not increase but it will not decrease, either.

Don't Test the Framework

You are more likely to succeed by leveraging the work of others than by duplicating their efforts. While you may find it fun to write your own <fill in your own pet project>, chances are good that someone else with greater expertise or experience has already written it, and hundreds or thousands of people are using it. Or it may be available as part of the standard features or libraries of your language of choice.

Frameworks, libraries, plug-ins, code generators, and their kin increasingly let us work at a higher and higher level of abstraction. Whether built in, commercial, or open source, we incorporate them into our development ecosystem and trust them to work correctly.

Commercial software comes with support and maintenance as well as—despite the license disclaimers—some expectation of fitness for

---

4. I refer to "features" here because coverage is not just about lines or statements. A thorough testing regimen may also consider branches, conditions, loop iterations, def-use chains, or other measurable features of the code.

purpose. The same is usually true of our system libraries, often including the backing design and support of a standards body in their design and specification. Open-source software comes with user communities and often includes test suites as part of their build and installation.

Generally, you do not need to test third-party code. I have lost count of the number of times I have seen developers, myself included, quickly jump to the conclusion that the compiler or library had a bug because it could not have been our mistake, only to realize after a long side trip that we should look at our own code first. Sure, sometimes shortcomings in the availability or quality of documentation contribute. Once in awhile, the bug really is in the third-party code. However, most of the problems are ours.

Someone else has done the work to guarantee the quality of the software. Let's not duplicate their efforts.

Don't Test Generated Code

Note that generated code also falls into this category. The benefits of generating source code have proven themselves for decades. Early compilers were assembly code generators. Many compilers are generated from descriptions of their lexemes and grammars. XML parsers, regular expression generators, and CORBA, SOAP, and REST interfaces all use code generation in many implementations. Trends toward domain-specific languages (DSLs) and higher-level constructs frequently employ generators, at least in their early incarnations. So why wouldn't we test that code?

First of all, code generation usually derives from a solid theoretical or experiential foundation. The generators implement empirically or algorithmically correct approaches to solve the problem. While this does not guarantee a correct implementation, it provides a solid basis for more proven solutions.

Second, generated code often solves problems for which the authors or the industry have not come up with generalized implementations. This means that the generated code is usually repetitious and is thus tedious to test.

Finally, I have found that much generated code ignores many good design principles, making it difficult to test. Many of the theory-based generators come from procedural heritages and do not share the same level of obsession with small functions that we see in current programming paradigms. And the code is simply not designed for human maintenance.

Test that you have used the generator to correctly achieve the purpose for your system. If you are using a compiler generator, make sure the generated compiler accepts the language you are trying to implement. For a remote API, test the business purpose of the API via the generated stubs.

Sometimes Test the Framework

To every rule, there are exceptions. When we talked about frameworks, we talked about things like trust, having tests, guarantees, and correctness. Sometimes, those conditions are not true. Other times, you cannot afford to assume they are true. Let's look at some times in which you need to test the framework.

Imagine you are part of a team working on a large software system, perhaps a product consisting of millions of lines of code, hundreds of developers, and using hundreds of third-party packages across the entire code base. In any given period of time between releases, perhaps dozens of those packages change and may need to be upgraded. How do you update the packages safely without breaking your system? You can rely on the tests you have written for your own use of the packages in part, but in other cases, particularly those in which you have chosen to stub or mock out the framework functionality (e.g., a service access library) or where it participates outside of the scope of your tests (like a dependency injection framework might, for example), your tests may not be sufficient to qualify the new version.

An open-source package without tests, especially one that is young, infrequently maintained, or with a history of incompatibility, also may not meet the standards of trust you need to include it without verification. Writing your own tests may be the most prudent course of action to ensure it meets your needs. You may even consider contributing your tests back to the project.

Frameworks with high-risk dependencies for your project probably also deserve greater attention to correctness. A simple framework used pervasively affects all parts of your system. A framework used comprehensively requires all parts of the framework to behave as expected.

In the end, testing third-party code entails a risk assessment of whether the cost of testing it justifies the benefits of reuse against the risk of failures. Consider it, and judge wisely.

Part II

Testing and Testability Patterns

With philosophy and principles in place, now it is time to dive into code, the essence of our craft. Part II starts with setting the basic foundation of consistency upon which to build your tests. It continues through increasingly sophisticated topics using examples from a variety of programming languages. It finishes with a discussion of how to test concurrency.

Chapter 6

The Basics

One of the hardest things about testing is sometimes just knowing where to start. This chapter focuses on just that. Starting with a class, we look at how you can provide a solid foundation for testing the rest of the functionality of the class.

Then we delve into some of the basic tools that can be used directly and are often used in more sophisticated testing scenarios. We examine structured ways to expose your hidden values and touch on topics that will be expanded in later chapters.

Along the way, we look at some of the variations available in the use of testing framework features. We also incorporate some of the test patterns from Meszaros's *xUnit Test Patterns* [xTP].

Bootstrapping Constructors

There is a basic dilemma in testing a well-encapsulated class that is so fundamental it is often overlooked: How do you know you have tested it correctly? You do not have access to the attributes of the class, so how do you verify that the constructor did its work correctly?

Sure, you can start with the most fundamental effect of a constructor and verify that a valid object was constructed. In the process, you also verify that no exceptions were thrown. But how do you verify that the internal state was initialized correctly (Listing 6-1)?

Listing 6-1: *Testing object construction and the lack of exceptions*

```
public void testMyObject() {
  MyObject sut = new MyObject();
  assertNotNull(sut);
}
```

If we didn't insist on strong encapsulation, we could directly query the attributes. However, we all learned on our first day of Object-Orientation Indoctrination that this is a Bad Thing. We learned that the only allowed way to access our attributes should be with our getter methods.

But wait, should we really use methods that have not been tested to verify the behavior of another method? Do we have any other choices? In short, we may—depending on the language—but none that are good enough to use on such a fundamental and consistent basis (Listing 6-2).

Listing 6-2: *Using a getter to verify constructor state*

```
public void testMyObject() {
  MyObject sut = new MyObject();
  assertNotNull(sut);
  assertEquals(expectedValue, sut.getAttribute());
}
```

Let's resolve this seemingly circular dependency before we proceed. The key to this apparent dilemma is to realize that in normal cases, it is sufficient for the constructor and the simple setters and getters to behave in a manner that is consistent with expectations. Essentially, we are saying, "If it looks like a class and acts like a class, it is safe to treat it like a class."

Which cases are not part of the aforementioned "normal cases," and what should we do if we encounter these deviations? Abnormal cases occur when the constructor initializes hidden state or the getters do more than simply pass the value of an attribute. In the former case, we can use techniques to give our tests privileged access to our classes, described in Chapter 9. In the latter case, I would suggest that the methods should be renamed to reveal their more complex nature and that they should not masquerade as getters.

A Mathematical View of Tests

For those who tend toward the mathematical, I have an analogy for tests that parallels two of the traditional approaches to mathematical proof. We are all familiar with the typical deductive proof. Given some set of fundamental facts or assumptions, we build a sound logical argument that leads us to a conclusion. As long as the initial assumptions are valid and the logical argument remains sound, we hold the conclusion as truth. System or integration tests are like deductive proofs. Given a set of initial conditions of the software, we apply a set of operations on the software and declare the software correct if the resulting state agrees with expectations. In fact, the given/when/then format[1] of behavior-driven development frameworks reinforces this interpretation. The tests generally stand alone. Collectively, they verify different aspects of the system that together serve to verify the whole system, ideally by covering all aspects of the system.

Unit tests are different. Unit tests may be seen as a deductive proof of the unit under test, but even that requires a bit of inference. The approach to bootstrapping constructors just described can be seen as the basis case for an inductive proof. Inductive proofs demonstrate the premise for a basis case and then demonstrate the inductive step: for any case n, the premise also holds for the $n+1$ case. Each step builds upon the next. Within the tests for a unit, the correctness of the more complex behaviors of the unit depend on the correctness of construction and basic attribute management as shown in Figure 6-1. In the larger context, unit tests for leaf components, those components that depend only on system libraries, are the basis case. Using the earlier heuristic of unit tests only testing the value added by the unit under test, each successful unit's tests provide an inductive step toward proving the correctness of the system.

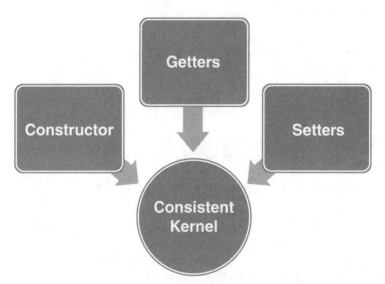

Figure 6-1: *A model for constructor bootstrapping as an inductive basis*

---

1. This has become known as the Gherkin format of test specification, deriving from its association with the Cucumber BDD testing framework.

In mathematics, both forms of proof are functionally equivalent and correct ways to support a conclusion. However, software systems are not mathematically rigorous systems. This analogy can serve as a useful model to differentiate the different approaches to testing, but neither is sufficient in and of itself to verify the system.

Testing Simple Getters and Setters

The bootstrapping dilemma applies equally to testing setters and getters, but the strategy presented in the previous section gives us a plan of attack. The encapsulation of the attributes prevents us from verifying the actions of the mutators without invoking the getters. It also inhibits us from setting the attributes to request through the getters without using the setters. Therefore, we are left with using getters to test setters and vice versa, effectively testing them together as shown in Listing 6-3.

Listing 6-3: *Testing setters and getters together*

```
1 public void testSetGetAttribute() {
2    MyObject sut = new MyObject();
3    assertNotNull(sut);
4    int expectedValue = 17;
5    assertThat(sut.getAttribute(),
          is(not(equalTo(expectedValue))));

6    sut.setAttribute(expectedValue);
7    int actualValue = sut.getAttribute();

8    assertEquals(expectedValue, actualValue);
9 }
```

First, note that the blank lines in the code divide the test into the sections of a Four-Phase Test [xTP] or, alternatively, the arrange-act-assert pattern. I find that explicitly delineating the phases where possible aids the clarity and legibility of the test. Even the introduction of the technically unnecessary intermediate variable actualValue assists in demarcating the phases and enhances the understanding of the intent.

The missing fourth phase is Garbage-Collected Teardown [xTP]. I highlight this because we need to be conscious of our teardown, even when the runtime does it for us. The prevalence of garbage-collected languages has simplified our code significantly by eliminating most of the overhead of explicit memory management. However, the corresponding removal of destructors has complicated the management of nonmemory resources—such as file handles and threads—at scope boundaries. In tests this applies to the clean up tasks we need to do at the end of the test for things that do not apply to all tests in a suite.

The use of assertions at lines 3 and 5 reinforces our preconditions for the test. JUnit provides a variant called an assumption, but it merely invalidates the test, treating it as if it were ignored. While this does not run a test whose preconditions have not been met, it also does not highlight that fact very strongly, so I will use assertions for this purpose instead.

Line 5 uses the more literate and declarative form embodied in Java by the Hamcrest matchers.[2] Notice how the statement of our assumption reads very naturally in a way that can be otherwise difficult in many xUnit variants with the absence of `assertNotEquals()`.

In the execution phase of the test, we invoke both the setter and the getter, accounting for the name of the test method even to the ordering of the verbs. We finish up with a standard equality assertion in the verification phase.

With these two tests in place, the verification of the constructor and of the setter and getter, we have "proven" that the basic foundation for the functionality of the unit under test is sound and consistent. This provides the basis upon which we will build the remainder of the verification of our class.

Share Constants

One of the challenges in getting started arises when constructors set state independent of getters and setters. A typical example of this occurs when constructors use default values, common when you have multiple constructors and simpler ones call more complex ones (Listing 6-4).

---

2. The Hamcrest matchers can be found at http://code.google.com/p/hamcrest/ and have been ported to several languages. They are included in the more recent versions of JUnit. Similar support for literate assertions is available for other frameworks.

Listing 6-4: *Use of literal default values in constructor implementations*

```java
public class FixedThreadPool {
  private final int poolSize;

  public FixedThreadPool(int poolSize) {
    this.poolSize = poolSize;
  }

  public FixedThreadPool() {
    this(10);
  }

  public int getPoolSize() {
    return poolSize;
  }
}
```

Testing the first constructor is trivial. We pass a pool size and use the getter to verify it. We cannot use the getter and setter combination test because the `poolSize` attribute cannot be changed once it is set. But how do we test that the default constructor does its job correctly? An initial attempt at a test might look like Listing 6-5.

Listing 6-5: *Testing a constructor that uses default values internally*

```java
@Test
public void testFixedThreadPool() {
  FixedThreadPool sut = new FixedThreadPool();

  int actualPoolSize = sut.getPoolSize();

  assertEquals(10, actualPoolSize);
}
```

This certainly gets the job done to start us off. What happens if the default pool size changes? As we have seen in previous examples, we get a maintainability benefit from coupling our test inputs to the expected values. The same is true with the "hidden" inputs that manifest with default values. Fortunately, we can easily refactor our code to make our defaults both visible and self-documenting. Review the refactored fragment of the original production code in Listing 6-6.

Listing 6-6: *Refactored code to extract default values to constants*

```
public class FixedThreadPool {
  public static final int DEFAULT_POOL_SIZE = 10;

  ...

  public FixedThreadPool() {
    this(DEFAULT_POOL_SIZE);
  }

  public int getPoolSize() {
    return poolSize;
  }
}
```

The declaration and usage of the DEFAULT_POOL_SIZE constant gives us a publicly accessible, intent-revealing name for the value used by the default constructor. Our test now becomes much more legible and less fragile when written as in Listing 6-7.

Listing 6-7: *Testing the constructor using a default value constant*

```
@Test
public void testFixedThreadPool() {
  FixedThreadPool sut = new FixedThreadPool();

  int actualPoolSize = sut.getPoolSize();

  assertEquals(FixedThreadPool.DEFAULT_POOL_SIZE,
      actualPoolSize);
}
```

The same technique can be used to expose string constants or even object constants and not just in constructors. Any fixed value or "magic number" that makes the software work is a candidate. You will often see such constants defined in well-defined libraries simply based on their convenience and readability, but they serve to enhance the testability of the software as well. This is a technique that is hard to abuse.[3]

---

3. However, like any good thing, it *can* be abused. The most egregious abuse I have seen of shared constants is the preallocated exception. In Java in particular, the stack trace for an exception is captured when the object is allocated. When it is preallocated as a static constant, the stack trace shows the static initialization context, not the context in which the exception is actually thrown. This can be very confusing when diagnosing a test failure.

Sometimes the form of constant values may differ. When there are multiple values that represent a fixed set, an enumeration is often used. Listing 6-8 shows a common idiom in C++ using nested anonymous enumerations.

Listing 6-8: *Using nested anonymous enumerations in C++ for closely related constants*

```
class 3DPoint {
  enum {
    X_INDEX = 0,
    Y_INDEX,
    Z_INDEX
  };

  ...
};
```

By default, the first member of the `enum` is assigned the value 0 automatically, but it is a common idiom to specify the initial value. Successive values increment by one from their predecessor.

Locally Redefine

Some languages let you redefine any variable or function within a scope and only for the duration of that scope. Let's say, for example, that we want to test a Perl subroutine that uses the `open` function. Consider how you might force an error in a test of the following line of idiomatic Perl.

```
open $fh, "<", "input.txt"
    or die "Could not open input file.";
```

The `open` function returns a nonzero value on success and the Perl undefined value otherwise. The short-circuit evaluation of the `or` evaluates the `open` as true on success and therefore skips the `die` statement. But how would we get `open` to return `undef`?

The test in Listing 6-9 shows how to use `local` to override `open` for the duration of the test and only within the scope of the test. Perl has block scope, so any reference to `open` within the block invokes the anonymous subroutine that simply returns `undef`.

Listing 6-9: *Using Perl `local` to redefine the open function within the test*

```
sub test_override_open {
  local *open = sub { return undef; };
  # Invoke the code that uses open
  ...
} # local definition of open goes away
```

Perl allows you to do this for variables as well as functions. The redefinition can happen regardless of the scope of the item being redefined. For example, the following line is used to turn off warnings from the `Archive::Extract` module only after the statement within the block that contains it.

```
local $Archive::Extract::WARN = 0;
```

This kind of local redefinition of symbols provides great power but is only available in a small number of languages.

Temporarily Replace

Some languages provide another way to test what code does without invoking the things that it calls. In the previous section, we showed a technique for locally redefining a function for the duration of the block, but the method will be redefined for all instances created from the module around the redefined function if you are using modules in an object-oriented way.

In contrast, JavaScript, with its dynamic characteristics and prototypal inheritance, allows each instance of an object to be independently customized. You can create an instance of an object and replace the implementation of its methods without modifying the behavior of the methods in any other instance (Listing 6-10).

Listing 6-10: *Simple example of replacing the `toString()` method of a JavaScript object*

```
var testObject = new Number();
testObject.toString = function() {
  return "I'm a test object.";
};
```

This technique can be quite powerful. The Jasmine test framework[4] has a `spyOn()` method that is used to capture and verify that a method was called, the number of calls, and the arguments for each call as shown in Listing 6-11. The `spyOn()` method wraps the original method in a `Spy` object that intercepts the call and records the characteristics of the calls before optionally calling the original method. The teardown automatically reverts the method to the original implementation.

Listing 6-11: *The Jasmine `spyOn()` method uses object redefinition to insert a recording proxy between the caller and the callee*

```
describe('Spy example', function() {
  it('calls toString', function() {
    var testObject = new Number();
    spyOn(testObject, 'toString');

    var result = testObject.toString();

    expect(testObject.toString).toHaveBeenCalled();
  });
});
```

Encapsulate and Override

A common operation in authentication, cache maintenance, and several other concerns is to expire an object that is older than some threshold. Listing 6-12 shows a typical implementation for an authentication token with a two-week lifetime.

Listing 6-12: *A typical implementation to expire an authentication token with a two-week lifetime*

```
public class AuthenticationManager {
  public static final EXPIRATION_DAYS = 14;
  ...
  // Return indicates if the token was expired
  public boolean expire(AuthenticationToken token) {
    Calendar expirationHorizon = Calendar.getInstance();
    expirationHorizon.add(Calendar.DAY, -EXPIRATION_DAYS);
    Calendar createdDate = token.getCreatedDate();
```

---

4. http://pivotal.github.com/jasmine/

```
    if (expirationHorizon.after(createdDate)) {
      authorizedTokens.remove(token);
      return true;
    }
    return false;
  }
}
```

A good suite of tests for this method would include tests immediately before, at, and after the expiration boundary. Let's look in particular at the test for just before the expiration boundary (Listing 6-13).

Listing 6-13: *Expiration boundary test for Listing 6-12*

```
public void testExpire_ImmediatelyBefore() {
  Calendar barelyValid = Calendar.getInstance();
  barelyValid.add(Calendar.DAY,
    -AuthenticationManager.EXPIRATION_DAYS);
  barelyValid.add(Calendar.MILLISECOND, 1);
  AuthenticationToken token = new AuthenticationToken();
  token.setCreatedDate(barelyValid);
  AuthenticationManager sut = new AuthenticationManager();

  Boolean expired = sut.expire(token);

  assertFalse(expired);
}
```

This looks reasonable, right? What would you say if I told you that this code has a race condition that makes it fail a relatively small percentage of the time? Do you see it? In some ways, this is a subtle variation on the "coincidental equality" described below. The sequence of events that triggers the test failure is as follows.

1. `barelyValid` is initialized.
2. One or more milliseconds passes while the rest of the fixture is created.
3. `expire()` is invoked, during which `expirationHorizon` is initialized to a value later than that to which `barelyValid` was initialized.
4. Comparing the adjusted values of the token's creation date and `expirationHorizon` expires the token.
5. `expire()` returns `true`, failing the test.

The **coincidental equality** is the assumption that the definition of "now" will not change between the initialization of `barelyValid` in

the test and the initialization of expirationHorizon in the implementation. The assumption that the time will not meaningfully change
even between adjacent statements occurs much too frequently and can
often be remedied with the Extract Variable [REF] refactoring in the
test. However, in this case, one of the initializations is outside of the
scope of the test, requiring some refactoring of the implementation.

Let's replace the initialization of expirationHorizon with a call
to the following method by application of the Extract Method [REF]
refactoring (see Listing 6-14).

Listing 6-14: *Refactoring initialization of the expiration horizon for testability*

```
protected Calendar computeNow() {
  return Calendar.getInstance();
}
```

We can now create a nested class in our test class that we will use
instead of the real AuthenticationManager and rewrite our test, as
shown in Listing 6-15.

Listing 6-15: *Rewriting the test from Listing 6-13 to use our refactored code*

```
private class TimeFrozenAuthenticationManager
    extends AuthenticationManager {
  private final Calendar now;
  public TimeFrozenAuthenticationManager(Calendar now) {
    this.now = now;
  }

  @Override
  protected Calendar computeNow() {
    return now.clone();
  }
};

public void testExpire_ImmediatelyBefore() {
  Calendar now = Calendar.getInstance();
  Calendar barelyValid = now.clone();
  barelyValid.add(Calendar.DAY,
    -AuthenticationManager.EXPIRATION_DAYS);
  barelyValid.add(Calendar.MILLISECOND, 1);
  AuthenticationToken token = new AuthenticationToken();
  token.setCreatedDate(barelyValid);
  AuthenticationManager sut =
      new TimeFrozenAuthenticationManager(now);

  Boolean expired = sut.expire(token);

  assertFalse(expired);
}
```

By encapsulating the invocation of an otherwise nonoverrideable system class, we have introduced the ability to freeze our expiration algorithm in time, making it easily testable. With the addition of some documentation or annotation-based infrastructure, we can suggest or enforce that the `computeNow()`[5] method should only be called from tests. We have traded a small amount of restricted access to internal state for a high degree of testability. The approach of encapsulating and overriding is one of the most common tools in unit testing. Often the encapsulation is already part of the implementation.

Adjust Visibility

Many of the things we have learned about encapsulation of software designs do not account for testability. We are encouraged to make things private, to provide access through methods, and to wrap behaviors in extra levels of indirection. While most of these heuristics, designs, and patterns suggest best practices and provide useful abstractions, very few account for the means and mechanisms to test them thoroughly.

Take simple procedural decomposition within a class, for example. Breaking an interface method into logical, purposeful submethods involves the creation of private methods according to the guidelines of encapsulation. However, if these submethods are as logical and purposeful as they should be, then they are also excellent candidates for direct testing to simplify the validation of the whole method that calls them.

Direct testing requires visibility outside of the class or at least techniques for breaking the encapsulation of the class. In languages like Java, encapsulation can be broken, security configuration permitting, through reflection. In some of the more dynamic languages, weak encapsulation is a language feature or, as in Perl, encapsulation is more of

---

5. I prefer to name the method `computeNow()` instead of `getNow()` so that the semantics of getters are exclusively associated with the get prefix. As systems grow, methods change in ways that are not anticipated. Rigorous adherence to the semantics for naming helps stave off some types of technical debt. As an example, I once worked with a system that used get methods to fetch complex objects from a database. As the system grew, the act of fetching had consequences requiring additional database writes, turning the get methods into methods that set as well.

an afterthought and can be broken more easily. Regardless, even the easiest of encapsulation-breaking techniques is uglier and more cumbersome than direct invocation.

We will examine several techniques for adjusting visibility in a later chapter. For now, let's look at an example in which we simply relax the strength of the ideal encapsulation. Consider a conventional data export method in Java (Listing 6-16).

Listing 6-16: *A hypothetical data export method*

```
public DataExport exportData(Search parameters, Format cues) {
  RawData raw = retrieveData(parameters);
  PreparedData prepared = prepareData(raw);
  return formatData(prepared, cues);
}

private RawData retrieveData(Search parameters) {
  ...
}

private PreparedData prepareData(RawData raw) {
  ...
}

private DataExport formatData(PreparedData prepared,
    Format cues) {
  ...
}
```

The `exportData()` method reads cleanly. The flow explains itself in a logical progression. Each of the submethods is encapsulated in a way that hides the implementation details from the client code. In doing so, the tests, which are also client code, must potentially perform a lot of fixture set up to test all three steps of the export.

For those not well versed in Java, Java has the concept of a package. Packages provide not just an organizational structure and a namespace, but classes that share a package also have certain access advantages between each other beyond those of classes in different packages. Specifically, a method[6] without an access modifier (i.e., no `public`, `private`, or `protected`) has "package default" visibility. Any class in the same package can access and invoke that method. An often over-

_____

6. Or member variable, for that matter, but we don't do direct variable access, right?

looked property of the `protected` modifier is that it is also accessible by other classes in the package.

In the previous example, either removing the `private` access modifiers from the three submethods or changing them to `protected`[7] would make those methods accessible from other classes in the package. Using `protected` would also facilitate the Encapsulate and Override strategy discussed earlier. In Java and many other languages, the same package can be used in different physical source trees, making it easy—and, in fact, standard practice—to segregate the tests but put them in the same package for ease of access.

This simple change weakens the encapsulation of the class a little, primarily for other closely related classes, but immensely increases the testability of the class. I prefer to think of these adjustments to conventional practice as pragmatic engineering alterations in support of the increased quality from testing. Perhaps the next generation of languages will have testing support built in so that we do not have to make these compromises.

Verification by Injection

All but the outermost components of our system—the leaf components—rely on other components to accomplish their tasks. These other components are called **collaborators**, or Depended-On Components (DOCs) in Meszaros's terminology [xTP]. Whether writing unit tests that test only the value added or when testing an integrated system, you often need to create substitutes for collaborators, known as **test doubles**. Especially at the unit level, injection is the most common way to introduce test doubles.

Generally speaking, dependency injection is the software-design pattern in which collaborators are inserted (i.e., injected) at runtime to satisfy the needed functionality. When testing, we can leverage various forms of dependency injection to insert mocks or stubs or simply to sever a heavyweight, time-consuming, or otherwise inconvenient dependency.

---

7. Personally, I prefer to use `protected`. One of the things I like least about Java is that the omission of a syntactic marker, the access modifier, has functional ramifications. I would much prefer if, for example, the `package` keyword were overloaded to explicitly denote package access.

Let's look at a simple example of testing by dependency injection. We will examine a wide variety of techniques for dependency injection later in Chapter 12. Imagine we are writing a system to manage a cluster of compute servers. Part of our allocation algorithm depends on the CPU load of the server. The code to determine whether a remote CPU is still within our allocation threshold might look like Listing 6-17.

Listing 6-17: *Code to determine whether a remote CPU is within a certain threshold*

```
class CPUManager {
  private final HostConnection connection;
  private int warningThreshold; // Percent

  public CPUManager(HostConnection connection,
      int warningThreshold) {
    this.connection = connection;
    this.warningThreshold = warningThreshold;
  }

  public boolean isHostUnderThreshold()
      throws RemoteException {
    // May throw RemoteException
    int load = connection.getCPULoad();
    return load < warningThreshold;
  }
}
```

Obviously, this class would have more methods than this—at least a setter and two getters and likely much more functionality—but this is sufficient to illustrate basic dependency injection. The declaration that `HostConnection.getCPULoad()` might throw `RemoteException` tells Java developers that it encapsulates a network connection. If we want to unit test this class, a network connection—not to mention the assumption of the machine it might connect to on the other end and trying to control the CPU load—would be very inconvenient.

But what if we could forego the network connection altogether and take control of the return from `getCPULoad()`? After all, it is not part of the value added by the `isHostUnderThreshold()` method. It is merely a source of data.

We can create our own version of `HostConnection` to test all the threshold variations, as shown in Listing 6-18.

Listing 6-18: *A custom* `HostConnection` *to inject threshold variations*

```
public class HostConnectionStub implements HostConnection {
  private final int cpuLoad;

  public HostConnectionStub(int cpuLoad) {
    this.cpuLoad = cpuLoad;
  }

  @Override
  public int getCPULoad() {
    return cpuLoad;
  }
}
```

While creating a test stub class might be overkill for a single variation, you can imagine testing for CPU loads below, at, or above the
threshold as well as tests for zero load and potentially tests for values
beyond 100% in the case of multiple cores per CPU. For several tests,
this is a useful class. Let's inject it into a test (Listing 6-19).

Listing 6-19: *Using a custom implementation to inject data values*

```
public void testIsHostUnderThreshold_Over() {
  int threshold = 50;
  int load = threshold + 20;
  HostConnection connection = new HostConnectionStub(load);
  CPUManager sut = new CPUManager(connection, threshold);

  boolean result = sut.isHostUnderThreshold();

  assertFalse(result);
}
```

With a few extra lines of code, we have constructed a stub that satisfies our functional requirements and avoids a network connection
and reliance on external hardware. By supplying that to the constructor, we have injected it into the software under test, simplifying a whole
category of tests for data variations. We will show ways to inject errors
and other behaviors later, in Chapters 9 and 12.

Chapter 7

String Handling

Strings are pervasive in computer programming. Whether joining names or generating or parsing XML documents, strings are a fundamental representation for much of the world's data, which leaves us with the task of verifying string data in our tests.

In this chapter, we examine several ways to verify strings in our tests. We start with the easiest and weakest approaches and increase the strength of our verification with little increase in the complexity of our approach. In the end, we have an approach that gives us strict verification yet is resilient to code changes and friendly to localization strategies.

Verification by Containment

Let's consider the code in Listing 7-1.

Listing 7-1: *A simple string composition function*

```
public String describeAddition(int left, int right) {
   return "The sum of " + left + " and " + right
     + " is " + (left + right);
}
```

While the example is trivial and a bit contrived, it is a fair representation of the way strings are commonly handled. How might we test such a method? Well, what do we know about the method? We know some fragments of the text, but those should not change from run to run. What we are probably most concerned with is that the correct values make it into the output. We might write a test like that in Listing 7-2.

Listing 7-2: *A test for the code in Listing 7-1*

```
public void testDescribeAddition() {
   int left = 3;
   int right = 5;
   int expectedSum = left + right;
   String expectedResult = "The sum of " + left
     + " and " + right
     + " is " + expectedSum;

   String actualResult = describeAddition(left, right);

   assertEquals(expectedSum, actualResult);
}
```

An ideal test will not break when trivial changes are made. What if we wanted to change the initial fragment to "The sum of the numbers" instead? We would have to make the change in two places, doubling the maintenance cost for that change. If there were multiple tests for the method—testing negative numbers, zero values, or special sums, for example—then the maintenance cost would increase severalfold.

I like to call the fact that the string in the test is the same as the string in the code "coincidental equality" or "coincidental similarity." We know the values are the same by construction. However, we have applied copy–paste reuse in a manner that increases the maintenance burden and fragility of our tests. There must be a better way.

Let's change our equality assertion to something more relaxed but at the same time less fragile (see Listing 7-3).

Listing 7-3: *Less fragile assertions for the test in Listing 7-2*

```
assertTrue(actualResult.contains(left));
assertTrue(actualResult.contains(right));
assertTrue(actualResult.contains(expectedSum));
```

Now we are resistant to changes in the initial string—or for that matter any of the string literals—but we have weakened the verification. We are only verifying part of the result. We have traded strength of verification for an improvement in the maintainability.

Additionally, what if one of our operands was 0? The expected sum would be the same as one of our operands. Or what if our operands were equal or the resulting sum had one of our operands as a substring, such as adding 9 and 1? The result of 10 would give us an ambiguous match against the operand of 1. In these cases, we would not know if the correct occurrence was verified by the assertion, leaving us with tests of unreliable value.

This technique can be useful and is certainly better than nothing. When using it, we should understand its limitations and use it judiciously. It can be particularly appropriate when the result is complex enough that a match gives us a high likelihood of correctness. If that is the case, we should be careful that we're not overspecifying the correctness by, for example, testing for containment of a string in which white space doesn't matter but our exemplar has a specific layout. Let's look at another approach.

Verification by Pattern

Just for linguistic diversity and because regular expressions are easier, let's translate our example to Perl. To show that some of our techniques apply outside of an object-oriented context, let's also make this procedural Perl (see Listing 7-4).

Listing 7-4: *Listing 7-1 rewritten in Perl*

```
package pattern;

sub describeAddition {
  my $left = shift;
  my $right = shift;
  my $sum = $left + $right;
  return "The sum of $left and $right is $sum";
}
```

Listing 7-5 shows how our original exact equality test might look like using `Test::Unit`, the Perl entry into the xUnit family.

Listing 7-5: *Listing 7-2 rewritten in Perl using Test::Unit*

```
use Test::Unit::Procedural;
use pattern;

sub test_describeAddition {
  my $left = 13;
  my $right = 17;
  my $expectedSum = $left + $right;

  $result = pattern::describeAddition($left, $right);

  assert($result eq
      "The sum of $left and $right is $expectedSum";
}

create_suite();
run_suite();
```

This test exhibits the same problems we noted before. We make hard-coded "assumptions" about the strings that join the numbers together. The test is not resilient to changes in the joining strings. How could we fix this in a nice, Perl-ish way?

One of Perl's strongest suits is the ease with which you can use regular expressions. Let's exploit that strength. First, we need to consider what we know about the expected result in a way that can be expressed as a regular expression, independent of the joining strings. Given the output that we know, we expect to have the first operand, the second operand, and the sum in that order and with some characters between them. Additionally, the sum is at the end of the result string. This lets us replace the assertion in the original test with

```
assert($result =~ /$left.*$right.*$expectedSum$/);
```

For those not familiar with the Perl regular expression operators, the =~ operator yields a Boolean result indicating whether the string on the left is matched by the regular expression on the right. We are asserting that $result matches the given regular expression.[1]

The net result is that we have verified that the values we expect occur in the expected relative order in the result string. This test is stronger than the containment from the previous section. We are now validating the presence of all three values in a manner that distinguishes them from each other with no chance of zeros, duplicate values, or accidentally nested substrings producing false positives. We might strengthen it a little more through the addition of whitespace, although we would add elements that are not necessarily an important aspect of the test.

---

1. If you're a little rusty on your regular expressions, the regular expression is normally delimited by the slash (/) character; the entire expression between the slashes is the regular expression to be matched. The expressions $left, $right, and $expectedSum are replaced with the values of our local variables in the test as literals in the regular expression. The dot (.) character means "any character." The asterisk (*) says "zero or more occurrences of the preceding pattern." Put them together and it expresses the "some characters between them" that we discussed. The last piece is the terminal dollar sign ($). Unlike the dollar signs that are used to denote variable references, the one at the end anchors the regular expression to the end of the string.

However, we still have issues with the maintainability of the test. It may be less fragile in the face of changes in the joining strings, but changes in argument order will break it. We have solved the "accidental equality" issue, but still have an "accidental similarity" issue. What would happen if we changed the phrasing to "You get 8 when you add 3 and 5"? Or what would happen if we internationalized the code and executed our test in a locale in which the natural word order would change? By the end of this chapter, we will have a solution for these.

Exact Verification by Value

Before we proceed further, let's apply a technique from Chapter 6 to our current topic of dealing with strings. One of the basic techniques was sharing constants. In our example, we showed how to use a constant for a default value in a way that simultaneously clarified the intent of the code and made it more testable. At the risk of stating the obvious, that same technique applies well to string verification—and not just verification of default values.

Let's look at the example of a web controller that, for reasons of compatibility, needs to translate URL parameters from an older version to a newer one. For brevity, let's assume that we only need to translate a single parameter and that we have a method in our class that deals with parameter translation (see Listing 7-6).

Listing 7-6: *Parameter translation in a web controller*

```
public class Controller {
  ...
  public String translateParameterName(String name) {
    if ("oldname".equals(name)) {
      return "newname";
    }
    return name;
  }
}
```

This is a simple transformational method whose outputs are strictly predictable from its inputs: an ideally testable method. Two tests for it are shown in Listing 7-7.

Listing 7-7: *Two tests for the code in Listing 7-6*

```
@Test
public void testTranslateParameterName_NewParam() {
  String expectedParam = "notoldname";
  Controller sut = new Controller();

  String actualParam =
      sut.translateParameterName(expectedParam);

  assertEquals(expectedParam, actualParam);
}

@Test
public void testTranslateParameterName_OldParam() {
  String inputParam = "oldname";
  Controller sut = new Controller();

  String actualParam = sut.translateParameterName(inputParam);

  assertEquals("newname", actualParam);
}
```

While these tests are intent revealing, they are not very resilient to change. For one, the first test makes the assumption that `expectedParam` is not the value that will be translated. We could remedy that with an assertion or assumption, but what would we compare it to? On the other hand, the second method suffers considerably from coincidental equality. Both the values of the input and the expected parameters are literal strings that (hopefully!) happen to correlate with the values in the implementation class.

With a quick bit of refactoring, we can improve the testability of `translateParameterName()` as shown in Listing 7-8.

Listing 7-8: *Refactoring Listing 7-6 for better testability*

```
public class Controller {
  public static final String OLD_PARAMETER_NAME = "oldname";
  public static final String NEW_PARAMETER_NAME = "newname";
  ...
  public String translateParameterName(String name) {
    if (OLD_PARAMETER_NAME.equals(name)) {
      return NEW_PARAMETER_NAME;
    }
    return name;
  }
}
```

That was simple, wasn't it? Two simple Extract Constant [REF] refactorings give us significantly improved testability. The strings in question were not private values in any sense. They were as public as possible when included in the URL for the request. Making them public constants of the class does nothing to break encapsulation. Now we can rewrite the tests to take advantage of the new constants (Listing 7-9).

Listing 7-9: *Refactoring the tests from Listing 7-7 to take advantage of our testability improvements*

```
@Test
public void testTranslateParameterName_NewParam() {
  String expectedParam = "notoldname";
  assertThat(expectedParam,
    not(equalTo(Controller.OLD_PARAMETER_NAME)));
  Controller sut = new Controller();

  String actualParam =
      sut.translateParameterName(expectedParam);

  assertThat(actualParam, equalTo(expectedParam));
}

@Test
public void testTranslateParameterName_OldParam() {
  String inputParam = Controller.OLD_PARAMETER_NAME;
  Controller sut = new Controller();

  String actualParam = sut.translateParameterName(inputParam);

  assertThat(actualParam,
      equalTo(Controller.NEW_PARAMETER_NAME));
}
```

By the addition of a precondition guard assertion[2] and by changing three literal strings to constant references we have added the ability to verify a precondition of one test and made both tests resistant to changes in the values being used. Now let's look at how far we can take this technique.

---

2. We are using the Hamcrest matchers for a more literate assertion style.

Exact Verification with Formatted Results

Going back to our example from Listing 7-1 with the `describeAddition()` method, even our Perl example left us with completeness, ordering, and localization issues. While these are less severe issues than the ones we started with, the increasing global reach and rapid pace of development make them suboptimal.

Let's recap what we have considered. Containment is weak and prone to false successes. Regular expressions provide a little more robustness but still have completeness and ordering issues. We could use constants instead of our literal strings, but this would not solve the outstanding problems if we only applied it to the joining fragments of the result.

But what if we consider a constant that can represent the entire result? Just like the URL parameters in the previous section, the text of the resulting message is not private, nor are the ways the parameters are inserted into the text. What if we could represent the entire result string with placeholders for the values we want to insert? That technology has existed at least since the C language libraries defined `printf` format strings. What if we refactored our method to take advantage of format strings as in Listing 7-10?

Listing 7-10: *Refactoring Listing 7-1 to use format strings*

```
public static final String ADDITION_FORMAT
    = "The sum of %d and %d is %d";

public String describeAddition(int left, int right) {
  return String.format(ADDITION_FORMAT,
      left, right, left + right);
}
```

We have not yet solved the ordering issue, but we have addressed the completeness and false-positive weaknesses of both the containment and regular expression approaches. Our test would now look like Listing 7-11.

Listing 7-11: *Format-based testing of Listing 7-10*

```
public void testDescribeAddition() {
  int left = 3;
  int right = 5;
  String expectedResult = String.format(ADDITION_FORMAT,
    left, right, left + right);
```

```
String actualResult = describeAddition(left, right);

assertEquals(expectedResult, actualResult);
}
```

But what about the ordering problem? Some languages and libraries, especially those designed for internationalization, have extended the C-style `printf` formatting to include positional references; Java has such positional references. Let's change the original implementation code as shown in Listing 7-12.

Listing 7-12: *Changing the implementation in Listing 7-10 to address parameter order*

```
public static final String ADDITION_FORMAT
  = "The sum of %1$d and %2$d is %3$d";

public String describeAddition(int left, int right) {
  return String.format(ADDITION_FORMAT,
      left, right, left + right);
}
```

The addition of the number followed by the dollar sign in the format string indicates the ordinal, 1-based index of the parameter in the argument list.

From this form, it is a small step to extract the format string to a localized resource file and make the constant the lookup key in the internationalization framework. Once these relatively simple changes are made, we have a test that can test our code regardless of the locale under which it is run.

Small changes in our implementation can make large differences in the maintainability and stability of our tests in the face of the inevitable evolution of our code base. We have gone from the weak verification of substring containment to a complete and change-resistant verification that even works in a multilanguage code base.[3]

---

3. Java has the advantage of natively working with UTF-16 strings. If you program in a language like C++ that requires use of a separate API for multibyte strings, the same techniques apply, but you will have to use the appropriate API, possibly convert representations, and maybe write some supplemental tools.

A Cautionary Note

The simple examples and tests in this section focus on string testing techniques. However, all of them resemble things you will find in production code at times. They also demonstrate the danger you find with simple implementations that the test's computation of the expected state may resemble the production code too closely.

By itself, this is not necessarily a problem, but it has a smell to it. Ideally, you should compute your expected result through a different algorithm than the implementation. This is the software-testing equivalent of double-entry bookkeeping in accounting. If you can arrive at the same answer by two different paths, you have a higher assurance that it is the correct answer.

The danger, and the source of the smell, is the temptation to just copy the implementation into the test or to write the test with too strong of a bias from looking at the implementation. This creates the most extreme case of verifying the implementation instead of the intent.

In the case of our string-formatting solution, there may not be another way to reasonably achieve the same result. Writing a string formatter from scratch or finding and using a different formatting library is overkill, yet there is just enough complexity to discourage performing an Inline Method [REF] refactoring if the method is used more than once or twice.

In the end, you need to test with intent. If you can write your test in a black-box approach, do so. If you cannot, ask yourself if there is a reasonable alternative way to compute the expected answer. If your fixture setup looks much like your production code, have a partner look it over to make sure the details are correct.

Chapter 8

Encapsulation and Override Variations

Chapter 6 introduced a technique to encapsulate functionality in such a way that we could override it for better control while testing. This chapter elaborates on that approach with several variations. We use encapsulation to create seams in our code that can then be exploited for verification. We also look at the use of test doubles (see the sidebar "Test Doubles and Interface-Based Design") to help us.

Data Injection

The simplest form of override encapsulation allows you to inject simple data into the software under test. No matter how much you model actors in your system as objects, attributes are still the fundamental building blocks. Let's start by using encapsulation and overriding with basic data types as shown in Listing 8-1.

Listing 8-1: *Code under test for basic data type injection*

```
public class TemperatureWatcher {
  public static final double REALLY_COLD_F = 0.0;
  public static final double REALLY_HOT_F = 100.0;

  public static final String REALLY_COLD_RESPONSE =
      "Really cold!";
  public static final String REALLY_HOT_RESPONSE =
      "Really hot!";
  public static final String NORMAL_RESPONSE = "Okay";

  private double readThermometerF() {
    // Read the thermometer
    return temperature;
  }

  public String describeTemperature() {
    double temperature = readThermometerF();
    if (temperature <= REALLY_COLD_F) {
      return REALLY_COLD_RESPONSE;
    }
    if (temperature >= REALLY_HOT_F) {
      return REALLY_HOT_RESPONSE;
    }
    return NORMAL_RESPONSE;
  }
}
```

This example demonstrates an interaction with the outside world, a perfect opportunity to use encapsulation to support testability. Interacting with the physical world includes a wide variety of interactions, like checking CPU load or memory utilization, taking voice or keyboard input, receiving data over the network, acquiring an image from a camera, or reading external sensors like thermometers or joint actuators.

With the encapsulation already done, we can adjust the visibility of readThermometerF() and use it as our testing seam by overriding it in our tests. We will vary our approach a little with this example. The mapping of the input to the output is easily specified as a pair of values, and we want to try several values in the range. We could write a test method for each data pair, but that would obscure that we are really executing the same test with different data. We could write a single test with a loop to iterate over the different data cases, but the loop really is not part of the test, just a mechanism we create to supplement the test framework. Instead, let's use TestNG[1] and its support for data-driven tests, sometimes referred to as table-driven tests (Listing 8-2).

Listing 8-2: *Test for Listing 8-1 using override injection*

```
public class TemperatureWatcherTest {
  @Test(dataProvider = "describeTemperatureData")
  public void testDescribeTemperature(
      double testTemp, String result) {
    TemperatureWatcher sut =
        new SoftTemperatureWatcher(testTemp);

    String actualResult = sut.describeTemperature();

    assertEquals(actualResult, result);
  }

  private Object[][] describeTemperatureData() {
    return {
      {TemperatureWatcher.REALLY_COLD_F - 10.0,
        TemperatureWatcher.REALLY_COLD_RESPONSE},
      {TemperatureWatcher.REALLY_COLD_F,
        TemperatureWatcher.REALLY_COLD_RESPONSE},
      {TemperatureWatcher.REALLY_COLD_F + 10.0,
        TemperatureWatcher.NORMAL_RESPONSE},
      {TemperatureWatcher.REALLY_HOT_F,
        TemperatureWatcher.REALLY_HOT_RESPONSE},
      {TemperatureWatcher.REALLY_HOT_F + 10.0,
        TemperatureWatcher.REALLY_HOT_RESPONSE}
    };
  }

  private class SoftTemperatureWatcher {
    private double temperature;
    public SoftTemperatureWatcher(double temperature) {
      this.temperature = temperature;
    }

  @Override
  protected double readThermometerF() {
    return temperature;
  }
}
```

---

1. JUnit has a similar feature that would be equally appropriate for our particular example, but I find it more cumbersome for most real-life examples. Look at the use of `@RunWith(Parameterized.class)` for details. While TestNG allows you to have the table defined per test method, JUnit forces you to define it per test class and runs the entire class for the parameters whether they use them or not.

The `@Test` annotation's `dataProvider` parameter says to use the data provider named `describeTemperatureData` to drive the test method. TestNG will find either a method tagged with that data provider name or a method by that name. The data provider method returns an array of arrays of objects. The arrays of objects must be the size of the parameter list for the test method and the data must be of assignment-compatible types.[2] Our data requires the temperature we want the thermometer to return and the expected response. Our data provider defines a range of interesting values, all expressed relative to the constants defined in the class.

The heart of the example lies with the `SoftTemperatureWatcher` class. We have defined a class whose constructor allows us to specify the temperature that would normally come from the hardware thermometer. It overrides the `readThermometerF()` method to return the specified temperature. Elevating the visibility of the method and the override are all we have to do in order to make `TemperatureWatcher` easily testable.

We can extend this approach in several ways.

Encapsulate Loop Conditions

Sometimes the termination condition of a loop is independent of the data being manipulated in the loop. One example occurs when you are looking for an external trigger such as an event, signal, or sensor reading to stop. Imagine you were writing the preheat controller for a commercial oven. Simplified pseudo-code for the initial heating cycle might look something like Listing 8-3.

Listing 8-3: *Simple pseudo-code for externally triggered loop termination*

```
while(underSetTemperature()) {
  keepHeating();
}
```

---

2. In Java, this pretty much means of or derived from the class type or type convertible using autoboxing, a feature that allows transparent conversion between plain data types like `int` and the corresponding class wrappers like `Integer`.

We have changed the problem domain slightly, but this example closely resembles the example from the previous section. The `underSetTemperature()` method encapsulates the logic around continuing to heat and returns a simple true or false. We can imagine that this method does something like reading a thermometer and comparing it to the set temperature to determine if more heat is needed.

Another common example frequently occurs in communication processing and in other types of processing that continue indefinitely or in which the termination condition is too complex for a simple conditional statement. In those cases, we have theoretically infinite loops (see Listing 8-4).

Listing 8-4: *Pseudo-code for an "infinite" loop*

```
void infiniteLoop() {
  while (true) {
    // Do something
    if (/* Some condition */) {
      break;
    }
  }
}
```

This form of loop can be particularly difficult to test. For one, it may be difficult to force it to terminate, leaving the possibility of an infinitely running test. If we are seeing strange behaviors that correspond to certain loop iterations, then the `true` condition inhibits our ability to control the iterations. If our code coverage requires us to execute zero, one, and many iterations of every loop, as you would have if you were using some coverage tools' loop metrics, then it is impossible to execute the loop zero times.

In all of these circumstances, we can encapsulate the loop condition, even if it is a trivial encapsulation of `return true`, to give us fine-grained control over the loop for testing purposes as in Listing 8-5. The simple override for the zero execution coverage condition would return `false` instead of `true`. The more complex override to test, for example, the fifth iteration of the loop would count the number of times it was called and return false after five iterations.

Listing 8-5: *Refactoring Listing 8-4 for testable loop control*

```
boolean shouldContinueLoop() {
  return true;
}

void infiniteLoop() {
  while(shouldContinueLoop()) {
    // Do something
    if (/* Some condition */) {
      break;
    }
  }
}
```

Error Injection

We can use injection to introduce the data of our choice for testing our software but we can also use it to force error conditions. Although best practice suggests that we keep our methods as small and as simple as possible, there are many times when the tradeoff against design complexity leads to a little more complexity in a method. Consider the hypothetical code to retrieve a response with a proprietary network protocol shown in Listing 8-6.

Listing 8-6: *Typical management of connection-oriented protocol in Java*

```
public class NetRetriever {
  public NetRetriever() {
  }

  public Response retrieveResponseFor(Request request)
      throws RetrievalException {
    try {
      openConnection();
      return makeRequest(request);
    } catch(RemoteException re) {
      logError("Error making request", re);
      throw new RetrievalException(re);
    } finally {
      closeConnection();
    }
  }
}
```

This kind of logic is typical of many connection-oriented protocols. In fact, it is a rather simple variation on one. For example, if you were retrieving a result set from a prepared statement using JDBC for database connections, you might have several things to clean up, including the result set object, the prepared statement object, the database connection, and possibly a transaction with commit or rollback paths.

Even in this example, several consequences of an exception would prove difficult to verify with the current code. As shown, there is no way to verify that the connection was cleaned up properly. Without knowing the implementation details of the logging, we do not know how easily we can verify the logging behavior.

But for the purposes of demonstrating error injection, let's look at what we can easily verify. We know that if the makeRequest() call throws a RemoteException, the method should throw an instance of RetrievalException wrapped around it. Listing 8-7 shows how such a test might look.

Listing 8-7: *Testing the error conditions of Listing 8-6*

```
@Test(expected = RetrievalException.class)
public void testRetrieveResponseFor_Exception()
    throws RetrievalException {
  NetRetriever sut = new NetRetriever() {
    @Override
    public Response makeRequest(Request request)
        throws RemoteException {
      throw new RemoteException();
    }
  };

  sut.retrieveResponseFor(null);
}
```

A couple of things might look strange here, especially if you aren't as comfortable with Java. First, the expected attribute of the Test annotation indicates that JUnit should only consider this a passing test if a RetrievalException is thrown. The lack of an exception or the throwing of any other exception constitutes a test failure. This allows us to specify that we expect an exception in a very streamlined way without elaborate try/catch logic cluttering the test. It has the limitation that it cannot verify anything about the exception, but for our purposes right now it suffices.

The construct we use to create our test object is called an *anonymous inner class*. It creates a class derived from `NetRetriever` that overrides the `makeRequest()` method. In a language like C++, we could create an inner or nested class for this purpose, but it would require a type name.

Finally, we do not capture the return of `retrieveResponseFor()` and we pass null to it. Neither one matters for our test's purposes. When a method throws an exception, it does not return a value; we are overriding the method to throw the exception from the method that would normally handle `request`. Our tests are only as elaborate as needed.

Using overrides to inject errors greatly expands the potential for our testing. Often, error handling code is the least thought out and least tested aspect. However, the grace with which your application handles errors and preserves a customer's work can make or break your reputation. Testing these error paths gives us an avenue to win the hearts and minds of our customers, even in the face of inevitable programming mistakes.

Replace Collaborators

A **collaborator** is a component your software interacts with. For our purposes, we care about the components that the component under test uses to accomplish its goal. Let's look at a reworked version of the previous `NetRetriever` example (Listing 8-8).

In a more realistic example, the connection would be managed separately from the `NetRetriever`. In addition to supporting the principle of separation of concerns, it abstracts the connection in a way that allows it to be reused and passed in from a larger context. While managing the open and close of the connection may not be the most neighborly or sporting approach in that design context, let's tolerate it for now.

Listing 8-8: *Listing 8-6 rewritten to pass the* `Connection` *to the constructor*

```
public class NetRetriever {
  private Connection connection;

  public NetRetriever(Connection connection) {
    this.connection = connection;
  }

  public Response retrieveResponseFor(Request request)
      throws RetrievalException {
    try {
      connection.open();
      return makeRequest(connection, request);
    } catch(RemoteException re) {
      logError("Error making request", re);
      throw new RetrievalException(re);
    } finally {
      if (connection.isOpen()) {
        connection.close();
      }
    }
  }
}
```

Now we pass a `Connection` to the constructor when we create a `NetRetriever` object. The `makeRequest()` method uses that `Connection` to make the request. The connection-management code in `retrieveResponseFor()` manages the connection more directly. Let's change our testing strategy to inject an error via the `Connection` instance rather than the `makeRequest()` method used in the previous section (Listing 8-9).

Listing 8-9: *Injecting an exception by replacing the* `Connection` *collaborator.*

```
@Test(expected = RetrievalException.class)
public void testRetrieveResponseFor_Exception()
    throws RetrievalException {
  Connection connection = new Connection() {
    @Override
    public void open() throws RemoteException {
      throw new RemoteException();
    }
  };

  NetRetriever sut = new NetRetriever(connection);

  sut.retrieveResponseFor(null);
}
```

Rather than override a method of the `NetRetriever` class, we have overridden a method of a collaborator and used that to inject an error into the method under test. In this instance, conventional design principles of encapsulation and separation of concerns have increased our testability rather than hindered it. The presence of an additional object to support the functionality of the class under test makes it easier to inject various influences—in this case, an error condition—into the flow of execution.

Test Doubles and Interface-Based Design

Injecting collaborators introduces the concept of a Test Double [xTP], a general term for the family of substitute components known as stubs, spies, fakes, and mocks. While you may hear many people use these terms loosely, Meszaros [xTP] usefully defines very specific characteristics for each.

- **Stubs** simply fill in for the collaborator.
- **Spies** provide after-the-fact access to the effects of the test on the collaborator.
- **Fakes** substitute lighter-weight implementations, often for test-performance reasons.
- **Mocks** fully record the interactions with the collaborator and verify the interactions during, as well as after, the test when possible.

Mocks—and mocking frameworks such as Java's JMock, EasyMock, and Mockito in particular—benefit from interface-based design. If you identify your collaborators through their capabilities as specified by their interface, the mocking frameworks make it easy to create mocks for you to inject. They have also made progress in mocking concrete classes, but the approach has limitations.

Dynamic languages like JavaScript are less tied to an explicit interface, although usage still defines a de facto interface. Jasmine's `spyOn` functionality provides the full range of test-double variations by substituting a test-instrumented recording object for the function being replaced and letting you define how it behaves when invoked.

In tests of the code in Listing 8-8, mocks are particularly useful in checking that `open()` and `close()` methods are called the right number of times to ensure proper resource management.

Use Existing No-Op Classes

In my opinion, one of the most underutilized of the common design patterns is the Null Object pattern.[3] The concept is simple. Instead of returning the ubiquitous `null` (or its various equivalents such as `undef`, `nil`, or `NULL`) and testing for it as a special value, we return an object of the expected type that implements the behavior associated with an unknown, missing, or indistinct value. Several such objects may reasonably exist for a given situation, giving rise to Martin Fowler's Special Case pattern[4] as a generalization.

Null object implementations are particularly useful in testing a stub. Take, for example, some code that passes an interface or abstract class as a parameter. What if the `Connection` used in Listing 8-7 were an interface instead of a class? To override even a single method we would have to implement all of the methods. In some languages, we could use a mocking framework like JMock, EasyMock, or Mockito in Java. Let's examine a technique we can use in almost all languages.

One can easily imagine `NetRetriever` as part of an overall application that could perhaps manage multiple connections. And this application might have the concept of a current connection, at least for the purposes of its user interface. How might one implement the current connection before an actual connection is chosen or even defined? Rather than use `null` and test for that special value everywhere as in Listing 8-10, let's create a `NoConnection` class that automatically initializes the current connection. This class would look something like Listing 8-11.

Listing 8-10: *An example of using null values to indicate error conditions*

```
if (currentConnection == null) {
  throw new InvalidConnectionException();
}
currentConnection.doSomething();
```

---

3. Surprisingly to many, this is not one of the original Gang of Four design patterns but was first proposed in the *Pattern Languages of Program Design* series. Martin Fowler [REF], Josh Kerievsky [RTP], and Robert Martin [CC08] all use it significantly.

4. http://martinfowler.com/eaaCatalog/specialCase.html

Listing 8-11: *An example Null Object pattern implementation of a* `Connection`

```
class NoConnection implements Connection {
  @Override
  public void open() throws RemoteException {
    throw new InvalidConnectionException();
  }

  @Override
  public void close() {
    // Who cares if we close a nonexistent connection?
    return;
  }

  @Override
  public void doSomething() throws RemoteException {
    throw new InvalidConnectionException();
  }
  ...
}
```

Now the conditional test for `currentConnection`'s null-ness can be removed. The `NoConnection` class behaves as one would expect a lack of connection to behave. In fact, in our example, it would behave much as a misbehaving connection might. Not only would this simplify our overall application code, it would also reduce the possibility of the dreaded `NullPointerException` that plagues many applications.

But there is an additional benefit for our purposes in writing tests. We now have a complete implementation of the interface as the basis for our injected objects. Using this null object implementation, the test from Listing 8-9 would use `NoConnection` as a stub (Listing 8-12).

Listing 8-12: *Testing using the implementation from Listing 8-11*

```
@Test(expected = RetrievalException.class)
public void testRetrieveResponseFor_Exception()
    throws RetrievalException {
  Connection connection = new NoConnection() {
    @Override
    public void open() throws RemoteException {
      throw new RemoteException();
    }
  };

  NetRetriever sut = new NetRetriever(connection);

  sut.retrieveResponseFor(null);
}
```

In fact, if `InvalidConnectionException` is derived from `RemoteException` as you would surmise from the `throws` clause in the method signature, we would not even need to override the `open()` method, simplifying our test to that in Listing 8-13. You could also derive it from `RuntimeException`, but should only do so if throwing a `RuntimeException` is a valid expectation in the context. Nothing in this context indicates that it is anticipated.

Listing 8-13: *Simplified test relying on our null object implementation*

```
@Test(expected = RetrievalException.class)
public void testRetrieveResponseFor_Exception()
    throws RetrievalException {
  Connection connection = new NoConnection();

  NetRetriever sut = new NetRetriever(connection);

  sut.retrieveResponseFor(null);
}
```

While this is a powerful technique, we should also be aware that it introduces coupling between our test and an additional production class. However, in the case of null object implementations, that coupling tends to be of little consequence.

Chapter 9

Adjusting Visibility

The ideals of object-oriented encapsulation generally steer us toward limiting the visibility of methods and attributes to the greatest extent possible and still satisfying the functional needs of the software. In general, this guidance is good. It lets us essentially virtualize our data elements so that all manipulation of those elements meets uniform expectations. Our most public methods represent the intrinsic behaviors that the outside world associates with the object being modeled. All other methods have lesser visibility motivated by their design purpose. Some methods are only visible to other classes—such as derived classes—of the same type. Different languages have additional variations in access levels.

For all the thought that has gone into the design of access levels in languages and the use of them to implement perfectly encapsulated software, very little of that thought addresses questions of testability. This leaves us with a situation in which we need to leverage the existing language features and relax the ideal encapsulations to enhance the testability of our software. This chapter introduces several techniques for adjusting visibility to improve testability.

Packaging Tests with Code

Many languages use packages or modules as a mechanism to help organize your classes. Many of these provide additional access privileges to code in the same package. Java has a special access level for things in the same package. Ruby modules provide namespaces and are the basis for mixins. Python modules are like classes, but its packages are purely organizational. But be careful. The Perl package declaration defines the name for the class not just the namespace it falls within. This difference is crucial as we will see in a moment.

The privileges of shared package membership give you access to more members of your software under test. Let's consider how this would impact the testability of the Java code in Listing 9-1.

Listing 9-1: *Packages and access level examples in Java*

```
package my.package.example;

class MyClass {
  public void runMe() { }
  protected void inheritMe() { }
  /* package */ void packageMe() { }
  private void hideMe() { }
}
```

Any class can access the `runMe()` method. On the other end of the spectrum, only the code in `MyClass` can invoke the `hideMe()` method. The `inheritMe()` method is most commonly understood to be accessible from derived classes. Code within the `my.package` `.example` package can invoke the `packageMe()` method and, as is often overlooked, the `inheritMe()` method. This last feature provides a significant level of support for testability.

With decreasing frequency, Java developers sometimes put their tests in a special "test" subpackage as in Listing 9-2.

Listing 9-2: *Putting tests in a special "test" sub-package*

```
package my.package.example.test;

class MyClassTest {
  public void testRunMe() { } // OK
  public void testInheritMe() { } // Not accessible!
  public void testPackageMe() { } // Not accessible!
  public void testHideMe() { } // Not accessible!
}
```

This is often done with the thinking that it is necessary to keep it separate from the production code. The Java packages correspond to directories relative to the root directories defined in the classpath. Since the classpath can have multiple directories, you can separate the tests from the code under test by putting them in the same package under different classpath entries with greater accessibility (see Listing 9-3).

Listing 9-3: *Putting tests in the same package as the software under test*

```
package my.package.example;

class MyClassTest {
  public void testRunMe() { } // OK
  public void testInheritMe() { } // OK
  public void testPackageMe() { } // OK
  public void testHideMe() { } // Not accessible!
}
```

We have now tripled our potential testing coverage simply by changing the package for our test code. Defining separate classpath roots for the test and production code allows us to cleanly keep them separate.

This approach does not work with Perl. Perl has a `PERL5LIB` environment variable that helps define a search path for Perl packages, somewhat similar to Java's classpath. However, the package declaration works a little differently, as shown in Listing 9-4.

Listing 9-4: *Package declarations in Perl work differently than in Java.*

```
package My::Package::Example::MyClass;

use Class::Std;

{
sub testMe { }
}
1;
```

This package statement declares not only the path from the root to the module, but the name of the module itself. Declaring your test in the same package would make it a part of the module, potentially changing the behavior of the code under test for all instances: a very undesirable trait in a test. Declaring the package with an extra component becomes essential to keep the test and production code logically separate, even if they are already physically separate in different directories.

Where the language permits, packages provide a useful way to give your tests elevated access to the code they are testing. The semantics of the language determine whether you can leverage that behavior in your particular programming environment.

Break It Down

Sometimes package access is not enough or is not available. Finding yourself unable to test tightly encapsulated functionality may indicate that your class is doing too much. Often you create private methods to simplify the implementation of the public interface. However, methods generally should be small. Your ability to functionally decompose a method into smaller methods of higher abstraction could mean that those methods constitute another class when taken together, particularly if they are reused.

Extracting your private implementation into a class can make it directly testable. Java allows more than one class in a file as long as the additional classes are not `public`; those classes have package scope. You can also make the extracted classes public for easier testing.

Once you have extracted the new class, you need to decide how to use it. You can make it part of the inheritance hierarchy or you can compose it within the original class and invoke it through that reference. Listing 9-5 shows an example of a class that can be broken up in both of these ways, and Listing 9-6 shows it broken up into three classes.

Listing 9-5: *A Java class awaiting refactoring*

```java
public class Car {
  public void start() {
    ...
    igniteEngine();
    ...
  }

  private void igniteEngine() { ... }
}
```

Listing 9-6: *Refactoring Listing 9-5 such that the separation of concerns enhances testability*

```java
public class Engine {
  public void ignite() { ... }
}

public class MotorVehicle {
  private Engine engine;
```

```
    protected void igniteEngine() {
        engine.ignite();
    }
}

public class Car extends MotorVehicle {
    public void start() {
        ...
        igniteEngine();
        ...
    }
}
```

Changing Access Levels

The next technique for adjusting visibility is the simplest in concept, but often the most controversial in practice. The simplicity comes from simply changing a keyword in your method declarations. In Java or C++, you might change `private` to `protected` or `protected` to `public`.[1] Java also offers package default as an escalation from `private`. In Perl's Class::Std,[2] you might change the `PRIVATE` trait to `RESTRICTED` or remove the `RESTRICTED` trait. You get the idea.

The controversy arises for the reasons alluded to in the opening text for the chapter. Software designers often choose access levels very carefully to capture the relationships between the entities being modeled as classes. A `public` method represents an intrinsic behavior for the entity as viewed by the world. A `protected` method represents "behavior" shared by all things of the same category or of the same type but which are not generally externally visible: essentially ways to alter higher-level

---

1. A programmer—one of the most talented I have known at just getting things to work—put `#define private public` in C++ before the headers of a third-party library to access members that were not otherwise exposed. Although I do not recommend using this technique, it was shockingly effective. I am not surprised that it compiled, but different access levels mangle their names differently at the object level, which should have prevented it from linking.

2. Damian Conway's Class::Std is one of several Perl object frameworks that have been created to compensate for Perl's inherent lack of objects. You can find it, like most everything Perl, at CPAN: http://search.cpan.org/perldoc?Class%3A%3AStd.

conceptual behaviors or to "configure" their type or instance. For example, all animals may move, but the ways in which they move vary greatly. `Private` methods are purely implementation details.

An encapsulation purist would say that these visibility levels represent a natural modeling of the entity and should be inviolable. While this may be a convincing argument for natural entities, what about all of the synthetic entities, such as data structures, managers, parsers, and so forth? These entities are implementations of theoretical constructs to begin with, most of which have multiple "natural" formulations that are functionally equivalent.

A slightly more pragmatic designer might acknowledge that we have established simplified semantic conventions for access levels, meaning that to have three or four levels vastly simplifies the spectrum of access variations in the real world; the real world is not even hierarchical. This designer might contend that those conventions should be followed for a variety of reasons.

Many of the reasons behind the conventions are sound. For example, I have yet to encounter a testing circumstance that required changing the visibility of private attributes. However, the structure presented in Chapter 6 for bootstrapping our testing is designed to avoid that visibility change.

Some of the conventions derive from a different context, however. The contextual difference that interests us the most relates to the resources for the running of tests. The principles behind today's object-oriented languages derive back to Smalltalk in their first commercially significant realization. Smalltalk started in the 1970s and was first made public in 1980. Personal computers were in their infancy and not very powerful. The general attitude was that computer time was more expensive than human time. As it pertains to testing, that means that test automation did not have a chance to be a driving force in the design of computer languages. In other words, access levels were designed without consideration for privileged access for tests.

I have now laid out a somewhat lengthy argument to allow the relaxation of "perfect" encapsulation principles to address the lack of explicit test access support in our modern languages. The chances are good that if you are reading this book, this makes so much sense you may be wondering why I wrote it. If you are not reading this book, then the argument may not sway you until the readers of this book buy a copy for you.

Once you have gotten past the rhetorical obstacles to changing access levels, the question becomes how to do it in the least damaging way.

Unfortunately, that recipe does not exist yet. However, when you relax the visibility of a member, I suggest you find a way to communicate that intent. Comments and documentation may suffice. In Java, several libraries, such as Google's Guava,[3] include a `@VisibleForTesting` annotation as an explicit indicator, although it does not enforce access.

Test-Only Interfaces

You can mitigate the exposure of changing access levels. You can introduce test-only interfaces to combine access level change with a weaker form of breaking down your class. In general, it enhances extensibility and testability to use interfaces as the primary types rather than concrete classes. From an object-oriented design perspective, this separates your definition of the behavioral specification from its implementation. Also, Java's mocking frameworks work best with interfaces, although they are getting better at handling concrete classes.

By using interfaces as the primary types, callers can only access the methods defined in that interface unless they have the bad manners to use the implementation class directly. This reduces the importance of the access levels of the noninterface members. However, you can further make the role of these methods explicit by grouping them into an alternate interface that the concrete class implements, as shown in Listing 9-7.

Listing 9-7: *Using a test-only interface in Java to help designate access-elevated members. Production code would refer to the* `Toaster` *interface, but test code could use the* `ToasterTester` *interface.*

```java
public interface Toaster {
  public void makeToast();
}

public interface ToasterTester extends Toaster {
  public void verifyPower();
  public void heatElements();
  public void waitUntilDone();
  public void stopElements();
  public void popUpToast();
}
```

---

3. http://code.google.com/p/guava-libraries/

```
public class DefaultToasterImpl implements ToasterTester {
  public void makeToast() {
    verifyPower();
    heatElements();
    waitUntilDone();
    stopElements();
    popUpToast();
  }

  ...

}
```

Naming the Unnamed

Many languages support the declaration of entities in a nested scope.
Java supports inner classes. C++ supports nested classes. JavaScript
lets you declare functions in just about any scope.

Several languages, including Java and JavaScript, allow you to
declare entities anonymously. In Java, you create anonymous inner
classes, commonly for simple or one-off callback classes like Swing
event handlers (see Listing 9-8). JavaScript developers pervasively use
anonymous functions as callbacks (Listing 9-9), for immediate execution, and to wrap function declarations to freeze closures.

Listing 9-8: *Example of an anonymous inner class as a Java Swing event listener*

```
button.addActionListener(
  new ActionListener() {
    public void ActionPerformed(ActionEvent event) {
      System.out.println(event.getActionCommand());
    }
  });
```

Listing 9-9: *JavaScript anonymous function as a click event handler in jQuery*

```
$('.clickable').bind(''click', function(event) {
  alert('Element has class(es): ' + event.target.className);
});
```

Anonymous entities are convenient to create, but difficult to test. They often have no visible reference in any scope external to the one in which they are declared. In many cases, the execution context dictates their signature (for functions) or interfaces (for classes). A simple Extract Class or Extract Method refactoring can bring anonymous entities into a visible scope with a name through which they can be referenced for testing purposes.

Becoming `friend`-ly

A relatively small number of languages have the equivalent of the C++ `friend` keyword. For example, Microsoft C# has the `InternalsVisibleToAttribute` class that can be used to grant access from specified contexts.

While many consider the `friend` keyword to be "dirty programming" and to violate principles of encapsulation,[4] it is often cited as having positive value for testing purposes, especially unit testing. Consider a C++ implementation of a poker hand (Listing 9-10), in this case in a simple game of five-card stud. Of course, you do not want to reveal your cards to anyone else.

Listing 9-10: *A C++ class with some justifiably private members*

```
class MyPokerHand
{
private:
  Card hand[5];
public:
  void receiveCard(Card& card);
  void layDownCard(Card& card);
  void evaluateHand();
};
```

While other players and the dealer should not see your cards until you lay them down, your test should be able to see the cards so that it can verify that you evaluate your hand correctly for play. By adding

```
friend class MyPokerHandTest;
```

---

4. You can find a good discussion of this at www.cprogramming.com/tutorial/friends .html. Scott Meyers infers something similar when he says, "It also eliminates the need for a `friend` declaration, which many regard as tacky in its own right" [MEC, p. 131].

to the MyPokerHand class, our tests can inspect the cards to make sure the playing strategy will win the wealth and riches we expect.

Coerced Access via Reflection

Java's reflection features distinguish it from most other strongly typed, compiled languages. Java reflection allows deep introspection and manipulation of types at runtime. Used judiciously, this can lead to highly capable generic code in production systems, although care must be taken to avoid the inherent performance penalty. You can also commit great evils with the power of reflection.[5] However, let's use it for good: to increase our ability to test.

Consider a simple class with only a single private method, as shown in Listing 9-11. In itself, this class is useless because the method cannot be invoked, but it characterizes the problem of testing private methods quite well. Regardless of whether it is private, a sufficiently complex or reused method deserves its own tests. Procedural decomposition encapsulates areas of logical functionality that can be independently testable, regardless of whether the functionality should be exposed outside of the class. By that line of reasoning, private methods are imminently testable.

Listing 9-11: *A simple class with a single private method*

```
package com.vance.qualitycode;

public class ReflectionCoercion {
  private int hardToTest() {
    return 42;
  }
}
```

How can we test this method? In addition to type introspection and invocation, Java reflection allows you to manipulate the accessibility of an element as well, through a simple yet powerful method on the

---

5. For some great examples of the evils that can be committed, see http://stackoverflow.com/questions/2481862/how-to-limit-setaccessible-to-only-legitimate-uses. My favorite part is making Strings mutable.

`AccessibleObject` class called `setAccessible()`. Subject to a `SecurityManager` check and some other minor restrictions, an argument of `true` makes the method accessible. In other words, a couple of simple reflection statements allow you to invoke the private methods of a class (Listing 9-12).

Listing 9-12: *Coercing test access to private methods with reflection*

```
public class ReflectionCoercionTest {
  @Test
  public void testHardToTest()
      throws NoSuchMethodException,
             InvocationTargetException,
             IllegalAccessException {
    ReflectionCoercion sut = new ReflectionCoercion();
    Method targetMethod =
      sut.getClass().getDeclaredMethod("hardToTest");
    targetMethod.setAccessible(true);

    Object result = targetMethod.invoke(sut);

    Assert.assertTrue(result instanceof Integer);
    Assert.assertEquals(42, result);
  }
}
```

First, we instantiate our class under test. Next, we use reflection to introspect on the method we wish to test. In a more complicated scenario, we may have to differentiate between different overloads of the same method name, but that is just a more sophisticated use of reflection. Ignoring the access level of the method is as simple as calling `setAccessible()`.[6]

This code would be awkward and repetitive if you needed to write it every time you tested a private method. Fortunately, several Java tools provide this feature in various forms, including dp4j,[7] PowerMock,[8] and Privateer.[9]

---

6. This can be restricted with a `SecurityManager`, but that should be easy to keep out of your tests.

7. http://code.google.com/p/dp4j/

8. http://code.google.com/p/powermock/

9. http://java.net/projects/privateer/

Declarative Scope Changing

Some of the more dynamic languages—I have used this with Perl in particular—allow you to declaratively change the scope of a block of code, much like reflection-base coercion. Although this features carries great potential for evil if you use it to pry open other people's encapsulation, we use it only for good. It leverages the general principle of using the rules of packages to give tests access to the code they are testing, doing so in a more targeted and purposeful way.

Let's look at an example using the Class::Std module for Perl object-oriented development (Listing 9-13). Class::Std lets you ascribe methods with traits that represent their visibility, much like the `protected` and `private` keywords in Java and C++. Using Class::Std, you use the `RESTRICTED` and `PRIVATE` traits, respectively. Class::Std uses Perl's dynamic reflection capabilities to intercept calls to these methods and to ensure the calls come from the appropriate scope, either from the class in which they are declared or, in the case of `RESTRICTED`, from a class derived from that class.

Listing 9-13: *A class with a private method using Class::Std in Perl*

```
package My::Class;

use Class::Std;

{
  sub some_internal_method : PRIVATE
  {
    # Do something the world need not see
  }
}
1;
```

If `some_internal_method` is sufficiently complex, it is best tested by itself rather than only through its callers. Its declaration as `PRIVATE` makes this difficult . . . unless we use our new trick (Listing 9-14).

Listing 9-14: *Using declarative scope changing to test the code in Listing 9-10*

```
package My::Test::Class;

use base qw(Test::Unit::TestCase);

sub test_some_internal_method {
  my $self = shift;
  my $sut = My::Class->new();
  my $result;

  {
    package My::Class;

    $result = $sut->some_internal_method();
  }

  # Assert something about $result
}
```

The **package** declaration within the test fools Class::Std into thinking that **some_internal_method** is being called from its own class. The surrounding braces let us restrict the declarative relocation only to the narrow scope of our call like good code citizens. Even if we choose to violate encapsulation for testability, we only do it for the minimum duration for which we need it.

Chapter 10

Interlude: Revisiting Intent

Chapter 2 discussed the topics of intentional programming and of understanding and testing the intent of code. Now that we have several chapters of testing techniques under our belts, let's consider a more complex example.

Everywhere you look, you will find code that mixes intentions together. Most often it begins because the responsibilities have not matured enough to warrant separation. It continues when developers fail to recognize that the concerns are crystallizing. This is all about the Single Responsibility Principle, the first of Uncle Bob Martin's SOLID principles.[1]

Sometimes, though, we leave concerns entangled because of idiomatic inertia—we have always seen it done that way, so we continue to do it that way—or because the implementation language does not support the constructs necessary to separate them. The latter occurs often when using design patterns. While the patterns themselves do not dictate an implementation, typical implementations have evolved.

This chapter will explore this kind of entanglement using the Singleton pattern [DP]. The Singleton pattern in particular is hard to

---

1. SOLID stands for Single responsibility, Open-closed, Liskov substitution, Interface segregation, and Dependency inversion. See [ASD] and http://butunclebob.com/ArticleS.UncleBob.PrinciplesOfOod.

test in its canonical form, so I will look at the testing options and the tradeoffs that need to be made to test it safely and effectively. I will then look at the general issue of separating concerns.

Testing the Singleton Pattern

The Singleton pattern guarantees uniform and controlled access to a unique instance of an object.[2] It acts as the object-oriented stand-in for a global variable in the cases in which such is warranted. In its purest use, it corresponds to a real and unique physical resource. It is often used to represent something that is unique to the application, such as an entry point to a remote service or an application registry.

There are several ways to implement singletons. A typical implementation in Java[3] is shown in Listing 10-1. Unlike in C++ or C#, you cannot create a reusable singleton base class in Java, so the language constraints result in continuous reimplementation of the pattern where it is needed.

Listing 10-1: *A typical Java implementation of the Singleton pattern*

```
public final class Singleton {
  private static Singleton instance = null;

  private Singleton() {
    // Initialization
  }

  public static synchronized Singleton getInstance() {
    if (instance == null) {
      instance = new Singleton();
    }
    return instance;
  }
}
```

2. Do not confuse the Singleton pattern with the broader concept of a singleton object, an object of which only one exists. The Singleton pattern is one way to ensure you have a singleton object, but there are other reasonable approaches.

3. With a quick search, you will find considerable debate about the "right" way to implement the Singleton pattern in any given language. In Java alone, the behavior of static member initialization and changes in the memory model with Java 5 fuel much discussion. There are similar issues in other languages, such as the C++ issues mentioned in *Design Patterns* [DP]. For the most part, these variations are not material to discussions about how to test singletons although testability may coax you away from some implementations.

```
public void doSomething() {
  // What the class does
}
}
```

Let's quickly walk through this. First, we have the class definition itself, which declares that the class cannot be subclassed, preventing the unique instance from being more specialized. Next, we have the class variable `instance` that references the unique instance of the class. The private constructor prevents uncontrolled construction of the class, making the `getInstance()` method the only, and thread-safe, way to obtain an instance of the class. Finally, the class has some additional methods to accomplish its purpose in the application.

Singleton Intent

There are really two purposes rolled into a single class for any given implementation of a singleton. The first purpose is clearly the implementation of the Singleton pattern characteristics. The second is the function of the class itself: the behaviors associated with the class modeling the singular resource.

Ordinarily, if we found such a clear duality of purpose in a single class, we would refactor it to separate the concerns. However, the singleton nature suggests that the separate intents live in the same class. The language issues around the behavior of class variables in inheritance hierarchies in most languages prohibit refactoring the singleton nature into a superclass without adding the complexity of a registry. Refactoring to a composition relationship exposes the construction of the class to some degree, contrary to the intent.

The Testing Strategy

Now that we have a handle on the intent of the singleton, we can focus on the value added by that intent. Given that we have two separate sets of intent, we can try to focus on testing the intents separately and hopefully simplify our testing problem.

A Word on Difficult-to-Test Designs

When you encounter a design that is hard to test, you should get in the habit of asking yourself whether or not there is a simpler, more testable design that will suffice. It always amazes me how much code can be eliminated and how much simpler a system can be when this question is asked.

One of the hidden and less recognized benefits of test-first approaches is the simplification to the system that occurs in the process. And when the production code is simpler and smaller, then the tests are easier to write and there are fewer of them. The net result is a system that takes less time to write and maintain and is less likely to contain bugs.

The Singleton pattern is a prime example. While the Singleton pattern enforces a single instance of a class, that enforcement may not be necessary with sufficient frameworks or cooperation.

Dependency injection is an excellent alternative to the Singleton pattern. By adding another argument to your constructors or work methods or by using the dependency injection facilities available in frameworks like EJB3, Spring, or Google Guice,[4] you can allocate a single object and use injection to ensure that it is passed around everywhere. This makes your object a singleton by convention or by configuration rather than by construction.

Eliminating the use of the pattern altogether is often the best way to make it testable.

Testing the Singleton Nature

Focusing on the singleton nature, there are two essential behaviors and two optional behaviors we need to test. The two essential behaviors are

- That getInstance() returns an instance of the class
- That getInstance() returns the same instance for all invocations

Let's address these and then talk about the optional behaviors. Note that we did not say anything about the initialized state of the instance. That is not part of the value added by the getInstance() method. Rather, it is part of the value added by the class member initialization and the constructor, which are a separate bundle of intents.

The second behavior, that the singleton always returns the same instance, is the behavior that makes singletons difficult to test. Why is that so?

---

4. http://code.google.com/p/google-guice/

The most common reason is that sharing an instance essentially forces us to use a Shared Fixture [xTP], whether we want to or not. While a shared fixture can be useful, a Fresh Fixture is always preferable to avoid test interactions as shared state is carried from one test to the next. Further, if you have tried to parallelize your tests on different threads, your shared instance will facilitate potential data collisions between the individual tests. All of this leads to Erratic Tests that will reduce your confidence in your test base and detract from your productivity as you continually diagnose and debug the failures.

To simply test the singleton behaviors, we can address this issue by testing both behaviors in a single test method (Listing 10-2).

Listing 10-2: *Testing the essential behaviors of a singleton's* `getInstance()` *method*

```
@Test
public void testGetInstance() {
  Singleton sut = Singleton.getInstance();
  Assert.assertNotNull(sut);
  Assert.assertSame(sut, Singleton.getInstance());
}
```

The optional behaviors for the singleton implementation above are

- The lazy loading behavior—that is, `getInstance()` only allocates the object on the first request
- That `getInstance()` performs its allocation in a thread-safe way

These behaviors are common to many singleton implementations. We won't address them directly here. Access coercion from Chapter 9 can be used to test lazy loading by providing access to the instance attribute. The thread-testing techniques from Chapter 13 may be used to verify the thread safety.

Testing the Class Purpose

We have separated the testing of the singleton nature from the testing of the class's functional purpose and addressed how to test the singleton nature. Testing the functional purpose is easy, right? It would be, except for one thing: we cannot construct an instance except through the singleton mechanism. The difficulty in testing the singleton's purpose is that we have no way to test it with a Fresh Fixture. The more tests we write, the higher the chances we will create Erratic Tests. So what are our options?

Briefly, our choices are to

- Remove the singleton nature
- Make no changes and live with testing a shared fixture
- Relax the constraints on `instance`
- Or relax the constraints on construction

Let's take a look at each of these options in turn.

The often least considered option is to simply change the design to eliminate the use of the Singleton pattern. Unless there is a significant performance motivation, you are creating a publicly visible API in which the control is important, or you are establishing an association with a single physical resource, you may not really need a singleton. (See the sidebar "A Word on Difficult-to-Test Designs"). Most of the time it is sufficient for the application to only create one instance and to support that uniqueness by convention and other mechanisms. However, sometimes singleton is the design of choice.

Living with the shared fixture may be viable for a short period of time, but it does not plan strongly for the growth of your test base. That leaves us with the options to relax the singleton constraints.

In general, relaxing the singleton constraints opens up usage possibilities contrary to the singleton intent. We are deliberately making the tradeoff between singleton enforcement and testability. We should select the alternatives that make the least egregious breaks in encapsulation and solve the most problems with testing singletons.

Relaxing the Constraints on `instance`

A commonly applied solution is to create a setter for the instance with restricted access. A typical implementation for the singleton coded previously might look like Listing 10-3.

Listing 10-3: *Relaxing the access on `instance` for testability*

```
protected synchronized

Singleton setInstance(Singleton newInstance) {
  Singleton oldInstance = instance;
  instance = newInstance;
  return oldInstance;
}
```

The method is synchronized to ensure consistency against the non-atomic test and set in `getInstance()`. Unlike a canonical setter, the method returns the old instance value. Because this method is purely in support of testing, returning the old value allows the test to reset it when finished. The use of `protected` explicitly specifies an access level that allows other package members to use it. We could also use the package default access level, but many code cleanliness regimens do not accept that for good reasons.

So we have created a mechanism that allows us to inject our own instance of the class, right? But wait. How do we create that instance? The constructor is private, so we cannot create one directly. The class is declared `final`, so we cannot derive from it. Either of these relaxations brings us to the relaxation of construction anyway, and the initial premise adds overhead to that.

We still haven't really solved our underlying issue, which is that of the shared fixture. We have added the ability to swap out the fixture and to restore it. That does not force any particular test to swap the fixture, guarantee that it will restore it, or prevent it from changing the fixture that it restores. And even though we have synchronized the fixture swap, that does not ensure transactionality with respect to the complete running of the tests, so threaded test runners will encounter race conditions.

Additionally, it creates the code smell Test Logic in Production [xTP]. We have added a method to our production code that is purely in support of testing without compelling benefit or protection.

This is not a compelling option.

Relaxing the Constraints on Construction

Opening up access to the constructor allows us to create fresh fixtures and to completely test the class's purpose independently from its singleton nature in a way that also supports concurrent test execution. The question then becomes: How should we accomplish this?

The general answer is: In the way that leaves us least exposed. The details vary depending on the facilities available in the language we are using. The tools we apply are those described in Chapter 9. In Listing 10-1, there are two primary options.

Using only simple changes to the code, we can change the access specifier on the constructor from `private` to either default (by removing it) or `protected`. The choice between them depends on your tolerance for the implicit default access scope. There is no need to make it `public`. If we put our unit tests into the same package as the class

under test, then we can access the constructor to create a fresh fixture
for each test as in Listing 10-4.

Listing 10-4: *Testing our singleton with relaxed access to the constructor*

```
@Test
public void testDoSomething() {
  Singleton sut = new Singleton();
  sut.doSomething();
  // Make assertions about the effects of doSomething()
}
```

An alternative uses reflection to coerce access to the `private` constructor. The code for this can be cumbersome and is probably best encapsulated in a helper method, fixture-creation method, or implicit
setup method. All of these have the side effect of making the code more
difficult to read and understand, but it may be worth it to preserve the
singleton encapsulation.

You can use the access-coercion techniques from Chapter 9 to rewrite your access to the private constructor with the reflection-based
coercion. This can work well if all developers running your tests use a
sufficiently uniform development environment, but it will raise barri-
ers to participation for code bases such as open-source projects.

C++ provides a more declarative alternative using the `friend` keyword. If a class declares its corresponding test class as a `friend`, that
test class has access to all private members. It does not provide the
fine-grained control exhibited by either access-level promotion or access coercion, but it preserves encapsulation better than the former and
leaves the choice to the implementation better than the latter. Simply
adding the line

```
friend class TestSingleton;
```

within the `Singleton` class will give the `TestSingleton` test class
full access to its internals. You could use it a little more surgically by
declaring each test method as a `friend` function, but that would be
harder to maintain over time.

The applicability of Perl's declarative scope changing varies depending on which Perl object approach you are using. Assuming you
are using a Perl OO approach that supports private construction,[5] it
can often be bypassed with code like that in Listing 10-5.

---

5. One of the more comprehensive Perl OO packages, Damian Conway's Class::Std,
does not explicitly support private constructors.

Listing 10-5: *Invoking the singleton constructor directly using package redeclaration*

```
package TestSingleton;
...
sub testDoSomething {
  my sut;
  {
    package Singleton;
    sut = Singleton->new();
  }
  ...
}
```

The Perl package name is almost universally the class name in Perl OO approaches. Assuming a convention of prepending `Test` to the package name for the tests, this code creates a subordinate code block in which it redeclares the package within that block, thus making Perl think that the call to the constructor is coming from within the class. If you are not used to Perl, you may have a slight sick feeling in your stomach right now, but we all make tradeoffs for testability.

Discerning Intent

We did a couple of things in this chapter. The obvious one is that we took a common—although sometimes controversial—design pattern and broke down how to test it while preserving the essence of its intent. More importantly, though, we recognized that some of the patterns we have been taught to use without question require closer inspection to test. To take this a step further, using accepted design patterns idiomatically—as a chunk[6] or out of habit—at a minimum complicates your testing—perhaps unnecessarily—and can unintentionally entangle concerns.

---

6. "Chunking" is a concept in the study of second-language acquisition. Effective language learners acquire "chunks," or sequences of words, as a unit rather than limiting their learning to the fundamental building blocks of the language. Often, these chunks are idiomatic, ritualistic, or difficult to parse, and can seem quite strange when used inappropriately or inaccurately. Increasing levels of abstraction and larger units of design such as design patterns are the chunks of the programming world, with the same benefits and perils.

You need to make sure any entanglement of concerns is fully intentional and justified by the costs. Your tests will show you where you have mixed concerns. Your fixtures will be unwieldy. Your tests will be long and complicated. Your tests may seem impossible to write due to that one seemingly important design decision.

When this happens, you have encountered a code smell through your tests. Your tests express or want to express an intent that you find hard to satisfy. You should consider changing your design and separating your concerns in a way that clarifies the intent of your code.

Chapter 11

Error Condition Verification

You can tell a well-written piece of software as much by the way it handles failures as by the way it implements its primary functionality. Software failures stimulate an inordinate proportion of the support requests against and, perhaps more importantly for your product's reputation, the blog posts, forum comments, and tweets about your product. Yet error paths are often the least tested part of the code.

This chapter focuses on testing your failure paths. It relies heavily on the material from the previous chapters. In fact, it adds little in the way of new techniques for verification and injection of behavior. Rather, it shows you how to apply the previous techniques to the problem of inducing and verifying the failures possible in your code.

Along the way, you will see ways to improve your error-handling approaches to make them more valuable and testable. The last section summarizes a number of design concerns toward that end.

Check the Return Value

The dominance of object-oriented design has not eliminated the use of the procedural models of API design. Use of and adaptation to older but ubiquitous procedural APIs such as POSIX suggest using returns and/or the global `errno` to communicate meaningful values corresponding to error conditions. Many POSIX calls, such as open(2),[1] return an integer −1 on error and use a range of errno values for the error details.

We have explored various ways to inject values into our code for testing purposes. We use those same techniques to inject procedural error codes. Commonly, we will thinly encapsulate procedural system APIs such as POSIX such that they can be overridden for error-injection purposes. At other times, we will use a heavier encapsulation—sometimes as an available library—to fully translate the error semantics of the return value into an exception-based equivalent that fits more naturally into an object-oriented design.

The remainder of the chapter will focus on exception-based approaches to verification.

Verify the Exception Type

As we showed in Chapter 8, the object-oriented testing frameworks make it easy to verify that a particular type of exception is thrown. Oftentimes, this is sufficient to determine the correctness of our code. Many methods only throw a single exception or only have a single error handling code path that requires testing.

The code in Listing 11-1 typifies a unified exception handling strategy in which errors are wrapped in an application-specific exception tailored to the context.

Listing 11-1: *A typical unified exception handling strategy*

```
public class SomeClass {
  public void doSomething() throws ServiceFailureException {
    try {
      makeNetworkRequest();
    } catch (RemoteException rexp) {
      throw new ServiceFailureException (rexp);
    }
  }
}
```

All RemoteExceptions thrown by makeNetworkRequest() will be wrapped in an exception specific to the context: in this case, the

---

1. See http://pubs.opengroup.org/onlinepubs/000095399/functions/open.html.

trite act of "doing something." You could convincingly argue that the value added by the error handling in this method is simply the wrapping and that the particular derived `RemoteException` is irrelevant to the operation of the method. In that case, verifying that a `ServiceFailureException` is thrown may be sufficient if `makeNetworkRequest()` cannot also throw that exception. The JUnit test for this code is in Listing 11-2.

Listing 11-2: *JUnit4 test for Listing 11-1*

```
@Test(expected = ServiceFailureException.class)
public void testDoSomething_Exception() {
  // Create fixture
  sut.doSomething();
}
```

The `expected` attribute of the `@Test` annotation tells JUnit to only consider the test as passed if an exception of the specified type is thrown. If another type of exception is thrown, or no exception is thrown, JUnit fails the test.

Using annotations greatly simplifies writing error condition tests. If you are using a language or framework without equivalent functionality, you may need to write the equivalent behavior yourself. Although the pattern is straightforward, some details are commonly missed when implementing it for the first time. Listing 11-3 demonstrates correct exception testing without direct framework support.

Listing 11-3: *JUnit test for Listing 11-1 with hand-coded exception handling*

```
public void testDoSomething_Exception() {
  // Create fixture
  try {
    sut.doSomething();
    fail();
  } catch(ServiceFailureException expected) {
    // Expected behavior
  }
}
```

We still rely on framework behavior to fail if any exception other than `ServiceFailureException` is thrown. If that functionality is not present, then use another `catch` clause with a `fail()` assertion.

The included `catch` clause deliberately ignores the exception we expect. The comment in the clause clearly communicates that this is the expected result; the comment will also suffice for many static checkers so they do not complain about an empty code block, something that I deem acceptable only in a testing context.

The key point that inexperienced testers often miss is the use of the `fail()` assertion in the `try` block. What would happen if the method accidentally succeeded without throwing an exception? Control would flow past it, out of the `try` block, past the `catch` block, and out of the method without encountering an assertion, resulting in a passed test. The additional assertion prevents a false positive result.

Verify the Exception Message

What should we do if our exception handling is not as simple and clean as in Listing 11-1? Perhaps we want to include a message with the exception that depends on the exact `RemoteException` thrown. Maybe we are writing an object-oriented wrapper around a procedural API and want to throw a different exception or include a different message depending on the error value. Listing 11-4 gives a simple example of the former scenario.

Listing 11-4: *Exception handling with multiple isomorphic exception paths. An alternative implementation would create an exception hierarchy from* `ServiceFailureException` *to distinguish the cases using techniques from the previous section.*

```
public class SomeClass {
  public static final String FAILED_TO_CONNECT =
      "Failed to connect";
  public static final String SERVER_FAILURE =
      "Server failure";

  public void doSomething() throws ServiceFailureException {
    try {
      makeNetworkRequest();
    } catch (ConnectException exp) {
      throw new ServiceFailureException(FAILED_TO_CONNECT,
          exp);
    } catch (ServerException exp) {
      throw new ServiceFailureException(SERVER_FAILURE, exp);
    }
  }
}
```

Both `ConnectException` and `ServerException` derive from `RemoteException`, as well as many others. Two suffice for illustration. How do we distinguish between the two variations of `ServiceFailureException` that the method can throw? Leveraging our prior discussion of string handling, we have prepared the code for the answer. The two things that distinguish the resulting exception are the message and the causal exception. For the moment, let's focus on the message.

The JUnit framework only provides direct support for expected exception classes, so we need to use manual exception verification if we want to verify details: in this case, the message string. Listing 11-5 shows how to do this.

Listing 11-5: *Verifying an exception message in JUnit*

```
public void testDoSomething_ConnectException() {
  // Create fixture to inject ConnectException
  try {
    sut.doSomething();
    fail();
  } catch(ServiceFailureException exp) {
    assertEquals(SomeClass.FAILED_TO_CONNECT,
        exp.getMessage());
  }
}
```

This is such a common pattern that some frameworks like TestNG have more explicit support for message-based verification. Listing 11-6 shows how we would write this using TestNG.

Listing 11-6: *Verifying an exception message in TestNG*

```
@Test(expectedExceptions = ServiceFailureException.class,
   expectedExceptionsMessageRegExp =
       SomeClass.FAILED_TO_CONNECT)
public void testDoSomething_ConnectException() {
  // Create fixture to inject ConnectException
  sut.doSomething();
}
```

This makes for a much clearer test. Not only will TestNG require that a `ServiceFailureException` is thrown, but the test will only pass if the specified regular expression matches the message. In our case, the regular expression is only a string constant. Relying on the full regular expression capability increases the power of this feature. In addition to the limitations noted in the section Verification by Pattern in Chapter 7, Java imposes further limits on the kinds of expressions that can be used as annotation arguments. All annotation arguments must be constants that can be resolved at compile time.

Verify the Exception Payload

We can generalize the idea of verifying the exception message. In the last section, we made a deliberate decision to temporarily ignore the cause of the exception, the other of the two attributes that could help us distinguish why the exception was thrown. We could have used the cause as an alternative means of verification or even to supplement our verification. In fact, the `message` and `cause` are the only user-settable attributes[2] of the `Throwable` class, the base class for exceptions of all types[3] in Java. `Throwable` closely resembles the base class of exception hierarchies in other languages and frameworks. For example, C# has the `System.Exception` class that has `InnerException` and `Message` attributes. C++ has only the `what()` accessor as equivalent to Java's `message`—but only definable by the class itself—and no cause.

Regardless of the language, exceptions are extensible. They can have attributes beyond those defined by the base system classes. While those attributes may not have an interface known to all, code that knows about the specific exceptions can reasonably know about the attributes. We will talk about reasons for and usages of extended exceptions later in the chapter. For now, let's simply assume they exist for a reason possibly beyond testability and examine them for testing.

In the test in Listing 11-5, we can verify the cause, or at least the type of the cause, simply by adding

```
assertTrue(exp.getCause() instanceof ConnectException);
```

inside the `catch` block. We have now verified that the cause of the exception is of the type we expect. This has the same shortcomings by

---

2. There are attributes that are only set by the system, such as the stack trace in Java and a more thorough description of the context in C#.

3. Java distinguishes between `Errors`, `RuntimeExceptions`, and other exceptions at a high level. An `Error` is a critical and unrecoverable system issue. A `RuntimeException` does not need to be declared and is considered a possibly unpredictable or unhandleable event. All other exceptions must be declared.

itself as verifying by type, as discussed earlier in this chapter. However, layering this on top of the verification of the primary exception's type and message verifies the primary exception more strongly. We can go further by applying all of our techniques for exception verification to the causal exception as well. In fact, we could drill down the chain, but we should keep in mind that the deeper we verify, the more we may potentially couple our test to implementation details inappropriately.

Java defines the `cause` attribute of an exception. What about attributes of our own invention? Imagine an API in an embedded controller for smart ovens with elaborate touch screen interfaces and user-friendly interactive displays. One feature of such an oven might allow the user to enter the desired temperature through a keypad rather than a dial. A dial has the concept of a temperature limit built into its markings and range of travel, whereas a digital display may only have similar inherent limits based on the number of digits in the display. Consider the subset of the oven's controller software in Listing 11-7.

Listing 11-7: *A subset of a hypothetical oven-controller API for a smart oven*

```
public class OvenController {
  private final int ratedTemperature;
  public OvenController(int ratedTemperature) {
    this.ratedTemperature = ratedTemperature;
  }

  public void setPreHeatTemperature(int temperature)
      throws IllegalArgumentException {
    if (temperature > ratedTemperature) {
      throw new RequestedTemperatureTooHighException(
          ratedTemperature, temperature);
    }
    // Set the preheat temperature
  }
}
```

We infer from this code that the `RequestedTemperatureTooHighException` derives from `IllegalArgumentException` because we declare the latter[4] but throw the former in the `setPreHeatTemperature()` method. But why did we supply the temperatures as arguments? Listing 11-8 shows a partial implementation of the exception.

_____

4. Technically, we do not have to declare `IllegalArgumentException` because it is a Java runtime exception. However, you *can* declare runtime exceptions, and in this case it simplifies our example. A more realistic example would use an application-defined exception as the base class.

Listing 11-8: *Partial implementation of the* `RequestedTemperature-`
`TooHighException`

```
public class RequestedTemperatureTooHighException
   extends IllegalArgumentException {
   private final int ratedTemperature;
   private final int requestedTemperature;

   public RequestedTemperatureTooHighException(
       int ratedTemperature, int requestedTemperature) {
     this.ratedTemperature = ratedTemperature;
     this.requestedTemperature = requestedTemperature;
   }

   public int getRatedTemperature() {
     return ratedTemperature;
   }

   public int getRequestedTemperature() {
     return requestedTemperature;
   }
   ...
}
```

The exception now carries detailed information about the reason it was thrown, information highly relevant to code that would catch this particular type of exception. This information also gives us a lever with which to more thoroughly verify the behavior of the software throwing the exception. Listing 11-9 contains such a test for our `OvenController`.

Listing 11-9: *A more rigorous test for the* `OvenController` *from Listing 11-7*

```
@Test
public void testSetPreHeatTemperature() {
   int ratedTemperature = 600;
   int requestedTemperature = 750;
   OvenController sut = new OvenController(ratedTemperature);

   try {
     sut.setPreHeatTemperature(requestedTemperature);
     fail();
   } catch(RequestedTemperatureTooHighException exp) {
     assertEquals(exp.getRatedTemperature(), ratedTemperature);
     assertEquals(exp.getRequestedTemperature(),
         requestedTemperature);
   }
}
```

Tying the input values to the error—as communicated via the exception—gives us a much higher coupling of inputs to outputs in our test and thus a higher level of confidence that our test verifies the software and exercises the specific exception path that we targeted. Exception payloads can consist of any data type, allowing rich verification opportunities. We will also see at the end of the chapter one of the ways that this testability improvement can also improve other aspects of our software.

Verify the Exception Instance

Each of the exception-based techniques so far essentially tried to infer the identity of the exception that we think should have been thrown by inspecting its characteristics: type, message, cause, and extended attributes. We have used increasing levels of detail to increase our confidence that we have identified the exception properly. You may have asked yourself, "Why not just inject the exception itself? Why not just use identity to verify identity?" That is the question this section addresses.

It almost goes without saying that identity is the strongest way to verify identity. But with objects—and particularly with exceptions—mutability and context are important.

Mutability refers to an object's ability to be changed. Some languages like C++ support pass-by-value semantics that makes copies of objects when they are passed as arguments. Otherwise, references are passed, and you can change the object through those references.

You may think this is not an issue for exceptions because they are generally immutable; their attributes should not be changeable after their creation or at least should not be changed. You also rarely pass exceptions as arguments, at least in the conventional sense; catch semantics usually pass exceptions by reference, analogous to argument passing by reference.

The most important aspect of exception mutability for our purposes, however, ties into the issue of context. In many languages, the runtime environment automatically inserts a lot of context when it creates an exception. This context differentiates exceptions from other objects significantly. Java includes a stack trace. C# includes several other attributes about the context as well, such as the application name and the throwing method.[5]

Unlike a constant of a fundamental data type like `int` or `String`, preallocating an exception for injection purposes immutably attaches the context of the object's creation rather than the context of where it is thrown. I do not recommend using this context to verify the exception. Inspecting the stack trace, for example, couples you very tightly to the implementation. A minor Extract Method [REF] refactoring can lead to Fragile Tests [xTP]. However, the testing frameworks will report the stack trace as part of the failure report in many cases, displaying misleading and ambiguous context for error diagnosis. A shared exception constant will show the same stack trace for multiple throw points: you will see a stack trace that does not actually refer to the place from which the exception was thrown. Additionally, a shared exception constant will show the same stack trace for each throw point when you have multiple test failures.

Now that we have considered the reasons not to use preallocated exceptions, let's look briefly at an example in which it is arguably justifiable. Listing 11-10 shows a slightly refactored version of our `OvenController` from earlier.

Listing 11-10: *A refactored version of our* `OvenController`

```
public class OvenController {
  private final int ratedTemperature;
  public OvenController(int ratedTemperature) {
    this.ratedTemperature = ratedTemperature;
  }

  public void setPreHeatTemperature(int temperature)
      throws IllegalArgumentException {
    validateRequestedTemperature(temperature);
    // Set the preheat temperature
  }

  protected void validateRequestedTemperature(int temperature)
      throws IllegalArgumentException {
    if (temperature > ratedTemperature) {
      throw new RequestedTemperatureTooHighException(
        ratedTemperature, temperature);
    }
  }
}
```

---

5. `Source` and `TargetSite`, respectively.

We have refactored the temperature validation logic into a separate protected method, allowing us to inject an exception through an override. Listing 11-11 shows the test for the refactored `OvenController`.

Listing 11-11: *Testing the refactored `OvenController` with a preallocated exception*

```java
@Test
public void testPreHeatTemperature_TooHigh() {
  int ratedTemperature = 600;
  int requestedTemperature = 750;

  IllegalArgumentException expectedException = new
    RequestedTemperatureTooHighException(ratedTemperature,
      requestedTemperature);

  OvenController sut = new FailingOvenController(
      ratedTemperature, expectedException);

  try {
    sut.setPreHeatTemperature(requestedTemperature);
    fail();
  } catch(RequestedTemperatureTooHighException exp) {
    assertSame(exp, expectedException);
  }
}

private class FailingOvenController extends OvenController {
  private final IllegalArgumentException toThrow;
  public FailingOvenController(int ratedTemperature,
      IllegalArgumentException toThrow) {
    super(ratedTemperature);
    this.toThrow = toThrow;
  }

  @Override
  protected void validateRequestedTemperature(int temperature)
      throws IllegalArgumentException {
    throw toThrow;
  }
}
```

We have used a preallocated exception to drive our result. Note that using it in this way presumes that the `validateRequested Temperature()` method is tested separately. Overriding the method as we do here prevents the original method from being invoked. We have avoided the pitfall of using shared exceptions with wildly misleading stack traces by creating a helper class that lets us define the exception very close to where it is thrown and as a nonshared object.

An even more compelling use of this technique would inject an exception that we would expect as the cause of a wrapping exception.

Thoughts on Exception Design

Before getting into the details of exception design, consider a facet that the simple examples in this chapter cannot communicate. Your overall exception handling strategy should guide the design and handling of your exceptions at the lowest levels. At least a napkin sketch of your exception handling architecture goes a long way to save you pain in the future. The following are some questions to consider.

- Will you handle exceptions at the top-most boundary layers such as UI, API, and service interfaces (my recommendation) or at lower levels in a more ad hoc fashion?

- In languages like Java in which the distinction is relevant, should you implement exceptions as checked exceptions that are declared as part of the method signatures or as unchecked exceptions?

- Are you allowed to swallow exceptions, preventing them from propagating, and if so, under what conditions?

- What are your strategies for converting or wrapping exceptions when the lower-level semantics become less appropriate for higher-level abstractions?

- Do you need to handle any exceptions differently, such as the need to handle `InterruptedException` in Java to deal with thread lifecycles properly?

Answering these and other questions will guide your exception design at the lower levels and minimize the confusion, inconsistency, and rework in your error handling strategy going forward.

Throughout this chapter, we have discussed various aspects of exception design to make exceptions and the code that uses them more testable. We have also identified or suggested a few additional benefits that we can derive from those same design considerations. Let's take a brief detour from testing implementation patterns to summarize the design elements that we can apply to make our exceptions stronger overall. An example combining these design elements is shown in Listing 11-12.

1. Derive exceptions from an application-specific base exception. All exceptions for the application can be caught without catching system exceptions.

2. Create a hierarchy of categorically relevant base exceptions. Exceptions that communicate similar semantic concepts (e.g., boundary errors) or that share common operational contexts (e.g., I/O operations) should be grouped in a unified inheritance hierarchy.

3. Use contextually specific exception types. An exception communicates a message about a failure condition. The exception's name should capture the meaning of the failure in a human-readable way, and the specificity of its type should make the failure programmatically isolatable and identifiable.

4. Use attributes to parameterize the exception's intent. Many exceptions correspond to situations that can be characterized by one or more data values. Capturing the values as raw attributes assists us in programmatically responding to the failure when necessary.

5. Exception attributes should only be settable through the constructor to the greatest practical extent. The characterization of the error should not need to change. Enhanced contextualization should derive from further enclosing exceptions.

6. Represent an exception's message as a literal format string constant. If no attributes are warranted, a simple literal string suffices. If attributes are present, the format string should format the attributes. This facilitates exact verification of scenarios involving complex string and data content.

7. If internationalization and localized error messages are required, the exception's message constant should be the lookup key for the format string. Bind the locale as late as necessary to localize the error for the context.

Listing 11-12: *Exceptions designed according to the recommended principles*

```java
public class MyApplicationException
    extends Exception {
  public MyApplicationException() {
    super();
  }

  public MyApplicationException(Throwable cause) {
    super(cause);
  }

  public String formatMessage(Locale locale) {
    throw new UnimplementedException();
  }
}

public class MyCategoryException
    extends MyApplicationException {
  public MyCategoryException() {
    super();
  }

  public MyCategoryException(Throwable cause) {
    super(cause);
  }
}

public ValueTooHighException
    extends MyCategoryException {
  public static final String MESSAGE_KEY = "value.too.high";
  private final int value;
  private final int threshold;

  public ValueTooHighException(int value, int threshold) {
    super();
    this.value = value;
    this.threshold = threshold;
  }

  public ValueTooHighException(int value, int threshold,
      Throwable cause) {
    super(cause);
    this.value = value;
    this.threshold = threshold;
  }
```

```
  @Override
  public String formatMessage(Locale locale) {
    String formatString = Dictionary.lookup(MESSAGE_KEY);
    return String.format(locale,
        formatString, value, threshold);
  }

  public String getLocalizedMessage() {
    return formatMessage(Locale.getDefault());
  }

  public String getMessage() {
    return formatMessage(Locale.ENGLISH);
  }
}

# The English dictionary entry for the message key
value.too.high = \
  The value %1$d is higher than the threshold %2$d.
```

Chapter 12

Use Existing Seams

Michael Feathers introduced the concept of **seams** [WEwLC] as a framework for bringing code under test. A seam in our code gives us the opportunity to take control of that code and exercise it in a testing context. Any place that we can execute, override, inject, or control the code could be a seam. Seams are all over the place. Sometimes, they are so obvious that we do not even think of them as seams. Other times, they are subtle or arcane and we miss them. And sometimes, we introduce them in order to be able to exert the control we need for testing.

Now that we have seen numerous techniques for bringing code under test, let's step back briefly and look at the big picture. This chapter roughly outlines an ordering of seam types within Feathers' category of object seams, but with some extensions to non-object-oriented programming models. The order in which they are presented roughly conveys the order in which I feel they should be considered for use in bringing code under test. The order considers factors such as ease of use and the inherent coupling to other interfaces, classes, or frameworks that the category generally entails.

Like any attempt to sort heuristics, the order should not be taken as a strict set of rules, but rather as a suggestion that can be overridden with reason. Additionally, this chapter suggests an order of consideration for *existing* seams. Changing an existing design for testability requires a far more complex set of reasoning than a simple hierarchy.

Direct Calls

Much like interpersonal communication, the direct approach works best but is often bypassed or overlooked. Hopefully, you do not worry about offending your code by communicating with it directly. Sometimes I have wondered when looking at the elaborate schemes people use for testing even when a direct approach is available.

Interfaces

For languages that syntactically support interfaces, the published interfaces are usually the best place to start. In addition to typically being documented, they tend to be the least coupled to other modules. They also have a high degree of stability over time, minimizing the effects of whatever coupling cannot be avoided.

In an object-oriented context, you would use the API published via features like Java's or C#'s interfaces or in C++ class headers. Procedural or functional languages might use function prototypes and signature declarations. Regardless, using the published API specification—even when testing implementations—helps to constrain your usage to the most stable portion of the specification. Even an unpublished, internal-use interface will tend to be more stable than an implementation.

Note that in a procedural or functional context, constructs like function prototypes and signatures fill the same role as object-oriented interfaces. Strictly typed languages like C provide stronger bindings and guarantees than the more flexible declarations in dynamic languages like Perl or JavaScript, but wide usage of loosely enforced interfaces still provide relatively strong guarantees of stability and compatibility for use in tests. For example, there is little need to question the jQuery event object's contents or to wonder how it will be passed to jQuery event handlers.

Regardless of the programming model in which you are working, you should favor use of the interface definition in your tests to the greatest extent possible when verifying implementations. This has the dual purpose of minimizing the coupling of your tests and helping to verify that your code meets the contract of the interfaces it implements.

Implementations

Almost by definition, you will not be able to test all of an implementation through its interface. All but the simplest of implementations will require nontrivial code to bring the interface's behavior to life. In other instances, an interface only represents a single role of an implementation class. Sometimes a class will implement multiple interfaces in this way.

You are less likely to encounter this phenomenon in functional or procedural languages in which the code under test has a single purpose. However, if you take a feature-based, rather than function- or method-based, approach to your testing, you may find the need to invoke multiple functions to test the feature, not all of which are part of a published interface.

Using the implementation and implementation-specific features directly is still a strong way to test your code. It provides direct verification of behaviors that are not accessible through published interfaces without incurring additional dependencies or fragile indirections.

Dependency Injection

Dependency injection[1] has grown from a hand-spun and somewhat obscure application assembly approach to a mainstream and widespread approach. Implemented in the Spring framework (Listing 12-1) and the EJB 3.0 (Listing 12-2) specifications in the Java world, Windsor container in .NET,[2] and others in many languages, use of dependency injection and inversion of control frameworks has become commonplace, if not always well understood. The prevalence of the frameworks and the principles behind them yields a high likelihood that we can use this pattern for our testing.

There are three widely accepted forms of dependency injection detailed by Martin Fowler and several less well-known forms, such as those available in the Yan framework.[3] Constructor and setter injection (both shown in Listing 12-3) prevail in the mainstream Java frameworks, and both are well supported.

---

1. Also known as Inversion of Control. See www.martinfowler.com/articles/injection .html for an early unifying treatment on the topic.

2. http://docs.castleproject.org/Windsor.MainPage.ashx

3. http://yan.codehaus.org/Dependency+Injection+Types

Listing 12-1: *Spring framework configuration of a service dependent on two other services. One service is injected using constructor injection, the other using setter injection. Note that "¬" indicates an artificial line break for purposes of formatting.*

```xml
<?xml version="1.0" encoding="UTF-8"?>
<beans xmlns="http://www.springframework.org/schema/beans"
       xmlns:xsi="http://www.w3.org/2001/XMLSchema-instance"
       xsi:schemaLocation=
          "http://www.springframework.org/schema/beans ¬
          http://www.springframework.org/schema/beans/¬
            spring-beans-2.0.xsd">
  <bean id="userServiceBean" class="..."/>
  <bean id="productServiceBean" class="..."/>
  <bean id="shoppingCartService" class="...">
    <constructor-arg ref="userServiceBean"/>
    <property name="productService" ref="productServiceBean"/>
  </bean>
</beans>
```

Listing 12-2: *Equivalent configuration to Listing 12-1 using JSR 330 annotations*

```java
public class ShoppingCartServiceImpl
    implements ShoppingCartService {
  private UserService userService;
  @Inject
  private ProductService productService;

  @Inject
  public ShoppingCartServiceImpl(UserService userService) {
    this.userService = userService;
  }
}
```

Listing 12-3: *Testing a method on the class in Listing 12-2 directly using EasyMock to mock the collaborators*

```java
import static org.easymock.EasyMock;

public class ShoppingCartServiceImplTest {
  @Test
  public void createCartWithProduct() {
    UserService userService =
      EasyMock.createMock(UserService.class);
    ProductService productService =
      EasyMock.createMock(ProductService.class);
    // Configure mocks
    EasyMock.replay(userService, productService);
    ShoppingCartService sut =
      new ShoppingCartServiceImpl(userService);
    sut.setProductService(productService);
```

```
    // Execute and assert something about the cart
  }
}
```

Constructor injection allows dependencies to be passed as parameters to a constructor. With this form, you declare all of the dependencies for an object in one place, but circular dependencies are not supported.

Setter injection relies on default constructors, and the object has at least a conventional setter to inject each dependency. Instances are created and injected as separate steps, permitting dependencies to be more flexibly resolved by the framework. With languages that support reflection, setter methods are not strictly required, although omitting them requires dependency injection support in your tests, as shown in Listing 12-4.

Listing 12-4: *Spring framework support for file-based configuration helps you inject alternate implementations when testing.*

```
package com.vance.qualitycode;

@RunWith(SpringJUnit4ClassRunner.class)
@Configuration({"test-context.xml"})
public class ContextTest {
...
}
```

The two forms of injection can be mixed in the same initialization, but the important feature for our purposes is that there are explicit parameter lists for us to use to inject collaborators for our tests. The forms that allow dependency injection also allow us to directly test the objects. Mocks are often used for the injected components to simplify the test double creation process.

The frameworks also provide facilities to inject collaborators using the injection infrastructure to simplify the construction of objects with many dependencies. In particular, the Spring framework supports this well.[4] It supports loading application contexts from files as in Listing 12-4 and, as of version 3.1, supports configuration classes (Listing 12-5). Both of these permit the injection of alternate implementations in the testing context.

---

4. http://static.springsource.org/spring/docs/3.1.0.M2/spring-framework-reference/html/testing.html#testcontext-framework

Listing 12-5: *As of version 3.1, the Spring framework supports configuration classes, allowing injected instances to be defined in the test code itself.*[5]

```
package com.example;

@RunWith(SpringJUnit4ClassRunner.class)
// ApplicationContext will be loaded from the static inner
// ContextConfiguration class
@ContextConfiguration(
  loader=AnnotationConfigContextLoader.class)
public class OrderServiceTest {

  @Configuration
  static class ContextConfiguration {

    // This bean will be injected into
    // the OrderServiceTest class
    @Bean
    public OrderService orderService() {
      OrderService orderService = new OrderServiceImpl();
      // Set properties, etc.
      return orderService;
    }
  }

  @Autowired
  private OrderService orderService;

  @Test
  public void testOrderService() {
    // Test the orderService
  }
}
```

Callbacks, Observers, Listeners, and Notifiers

Pretty much any system that requires a low-latency response to asynchronous events uses some form of callbacks, observers, or notifiers.

---

5. This example was taken from http://www.swiftmind.com/de/2011/06/22/spring-3-1-m2-testing-with-configuration-classes-and-profiles/ with the permission of Sam Brannen.

They can be found in user interface toolkits, in which they are often called event listeners, and distributed systems. Callbacks are a generic mechanism allowing you to supply code that the system invokes when certain well-known events happen. They have a variety of forms, some making creative use of language-specific features. Languages like C, Perl, JavaScript, and others with a procedural or functional flavor use function pointers (Listing 12-6) or function references (Listing 12-7). Object-oriented languages often implement callbacks through implementations of special-purpose interfaces as in Listing 12-8. Languages with reflection or dynamic invocation capabilities can provide callback functionality through strings representing the names of classes, methods, or functions; Listing 12-9 shows an example using the Spring Scheduling framework. In some cases, operating systems present language-independent reflection-like mechanisms such as the POSIX dynamic-loading APIs (Listing 12-10). C++ pointer-to-member-function syntax (Listing 12-11) supports a kind of type-constrained callback. C++ function invocation operator overloading allows the use of function objects, or functors,[6] as a form of callback as shown in Listing 12-12.

Listing 12-6: *Example from the Standard C Library[7] of an interface requiring a function pointer*

```
#include <stdlib.h>
void qsort(void *base, size_t nmemb, size_t size,
    int (*compar)(const void *, const void *));
```

Listing 12-7: *Callback functions are commonplace in JavaScript, such as in the use of jQuery.each() shown here.*

```
$('.menu > .menuitem').each(function(index, element) {
  console.log('Item ' + index + ' says ' + $(element).text());
});
```

---

6. http://en.wikipedia.org/wiki/Function_object

7. ISO/IEC 9899:1990 Section 7.10.5.2

Listing 12-8: *Java's Swing user interface framework defines a large number of listener interfaces, such as the* `ActionListener` *used here for a simple button response.*

```java
public class HiThere implements ActionListener {
  ...
  public void init() {
    button.addActionListener(this);
  }
  ...
  public void actionPerformed(ActionEvent e) {
    textArea.append("Hello, World!");
  }
}
```

Listing 12-9: *Spring Scheduling configuration for a reflection-based scheduling callback defined by strings detailing the class and method to be invoked. Note that "¬" indicates an artificial line break for purposes of formatting.*

```xml
<bean id="runMeJob"
    class="org.springframework.scheduling.quartz¬
      .MethodInvokingJobDetailFactoryBean">
  <property name="targetObject" ref="runMeTask" />
  <property name="targetMethod" value="printMe" />
</bean>
```

Listing 12-10: *Example of using the POSIX dlopen(3) API[8] to load and invoke a function from a shared library as a callback.*

```c
#include <stdio.h>
#include <stdlib.h>
#include <dlfcn.h>
/* For NAN macro */
#define _GNU_SOURCE
#include <math.h>

double
call_double_return_double(char *libname,
    char *funcname, double arg)
{
  void *handle;
  double (*func)(double);
  char *error;
  double result;
```

8. http://linux.die.net/man/3/dlopen

```
handle = dlopen(libname, RTLD_LAZY);
if (NULL == handle) {
  fprintf(stderr, "%s\n", dlerror());
  return NAN;
}

dlerror();    /* Clear any existing error */

*(void **) (&func) = dlsym(handle, funcname);

error = dlerror();
if (error != NULL)  {
  fprintf(stderr, "%s\n", error);
  return NAN;
}

result = (*func)(arg));
dlclose(handle);
return result;
}
```

Listing 12-11: *Using C++ pointer-to-member functions to implement a callback with a signature like that in Listing 12-11*

```
typedef double (Callback::*CallbackMember)(double);

call_double_returns_double(Callback &cb,
    CallbackMember cbm, double arg)
{
  return cb.*cbm(arg);
}
```

Listing 12-12: *Example of the base class for a basic C++ functor that takes a string as its argument and returns nothing. Using templates and pointers to member functions, you can create some very sophisticated generalizations of functors in C++. The Boost library supports creation of functors with combinations of* boost::function *and* boost::bind, *which were incorporated into the C++11 standard's* <functional> *header.[9]*

```
class AbstractFunctor
{
public:
  virtual void operator()(const char *string)= 0;
}
```

---

9. ISO/IEC 14882:2011 Section 20.8

Specific uses of callbacks have become known by more specific names representing their particular purposes. The Observer pattern [DP] uses callbacks in a specialized way to immediately communicate when a particular state or condition changes. Another specialized form of callback, the notifier, allows client code to register interest in specific events, often as part of a logging or monitoring strategy.

All callbacks have the common purpose of synchronously communicating various conditions to interested code. Often the conditions that are the subject of the communication are otherwise encapsulated. For testing purposes, you should even consider the invocation of a callback as a feature requiring verification.

However, this feature of the code's behavior also represents an exploitable seam. Callbacks usually accept data about the change or event that occurred. Callbacks also occur at well-understood times in the processing of the system that makes them available. More often than not, callbacks can be used to verify that the system handles and passes on data correctly, even when no other direct means is available. You can use mock implementations of callbacks for behavioral verification. You can even use them to exert control over test and thread execution, as we will see in Chapter 13.

Registries

Registries are lookup stores that allow specific values or implementations to be associated with a lookup key, typically a type of directory path, so that they can be looked up independently from different components or processes. Well-known examples include LDAP, the Windows Registry and Microsoft's ActiveDirectory, Java's JNDI with its various context interfaces like ServletContext and InitialContext, the Java RMI registry, and even runtime configuration files like those for Tomcat or Glassfish. To some extent even the venerable DNS and near-ubiquitous environment variables can be used as registries.

Registries usually allow their data to be organized hierarchically. Lookup stores like LDAP allow you to assign some degree of semantic meaning to levels of the hierarchy, such as the organizational unit (OU). Older registries only allowed the storage of values, originally as strings and later as typed data. In those systems, applications would use the values to construct resource locators. Newer systems also allow the storage of executable references, such as object and remote invocation references, so that the stored resource can be called directly without as much overhead.

The usefulness of registries comes from the ability to change them dynamically. When callable references are stored, you can replace a remote reference to a network-based service with a local object reference created by your test.[10] If the values are used to generate a resource locator, you can substitute values that reference a resource under test control or at least one that is known to be appropriate for testing. Registries make useful seams because they provide an indirect form of dependency injection based on mutually known information: the lookup key.

Another way to use registries as seams is to simply replace the registry implementation. Depending on the context, some implementations make this easier than others. The key difference typically surfaces in how you bootstrap the registry. If a registry is a way to find global resources and a registry is a global resource, how do you find the registry? In environments in which the registry can be defined by configuration, such as J2EE containers, new registry implementations can be injected with ease, shown in Listings 12-13 and 12-14. Less flexible environments access the registry through static methods that are hardwired and cannot be overridden.

Listing 12-13: *A basic servlet retrieving its* `ServletContext`

```
public class MyServlet extends HttpServlet {
  public void service(HttpServletRequest request,
                      HttpServletResponse response)
     throws IOException, ServletException {
    ServletContext context = getServletContext();
  }
}
```

---

10. This is a highly advisable strategy, not just to insulate your tests from use of the network but to protect your tests from interacting with each other both concurrently and sequentially.

Listing 12-14: *Using* `EasyMock` *to mock the* `ServletContext` *in a Java servlet. This approach safely intercepts calls into the registry representing the servlet's context.*

```
import static org.easymock.EasyMock.*;

public class MyServletTest {
  public void testService() throws Exception {
    ServletConfig servletConfig =
      createMock(ServletConfig.class);
    ServletContext servletContext =
      createMock(ServletContext.class);
    expect(servletConfig.getServletContext())
      .andReturn(servletContext).anyTimes();
    replay(servletContext, servletConfig);

    MyServlet sut = new MyServlet();
    sut.init(servletConfig);
    // Prepare a request and a response also
    ...
    sut.service(request, response);

    verify(servletContext, servletConfig);
  }
}
```

The same features that enable or prevent registry replacement are also liabilities when using registries as seams for testing. Even configurable registries are typically only configurable for an entire JVM or runtime environment. This introduces some of the same challenges of singletons in testing. At least in the context within which the registry is shared, there is the possibility that a misbehaving test could leave a substitute registry entry that would affect future test runs and that tests running concurrently could interfere with each other if they modified the same registry entries at the same time.

Factories

Factories generate entities on demand based on templated or predetermined initialization criteria. We most commonly think of the Gang of Four Abstract Factory [DP] pattern in this role. Other factories exist, including Factory Method and Builder [DP].

Each approach and implementation has distinct characteristics to satisfy its target use case. The key features for consideration in testing are summarized here.

- *Singleton-ness:* Is the factory a singleton that will, by its nature, be shared between tests?

- *Entity initialization flexibility:* Does the implementation have sufficient mechanisms to initialize generated entities for the necessary testing variations?

- *Registration management:* Does the factory allow generated entity types to be registered and deregistered dynamically?

The variations in these characteristics determine the degree to which a particular factory implementation is desirable for use as a seam when testing.

Many implementations of the Abstract Factory pattern are also instances of the Singleton pattern. The reasoning is that a standardized source of entity generation should be the only source of those entities. For many applications, this satisfies the usage needs but has the same testing challenges of all singletons; primarily, tests will share the instance and run the risk of interfering with each other.

Factory methods can suffer from this limitation as well. By nature of their definition, they are singletons; there will generally be only one instance of a particular method because they are typically static, and the data sources that drive their behavior need to be singular.[11]

Factories tend to have limited accommodations to initialize the entities that they create. The generalized nature of their role contributes to this; a mechanism that can generate a variety of entities needs to place sometimes-unacceptable constraints and requirements on those entities to initialize them consistently. Additionally, the need to create entities according to constraining requirements for their purposes motivates limiting the degree of customization that is allowed through the factory. While limited initialization of created entities may fit well within the design goals of the application, it can limit our ability to test the behavior of the factory.

Many applications statically configure their factories with the templates and instances necessary for their runtime behavior. Statically configured factories tightly couple your code to the types and implementations of the created entities, leading to undesirable coupling of the tests. Factories that support dynamic registration of created entities

---

11. Note that some languages provide features that can mitigate these concerns. Using `local` in Perl to override subroutine definitions or substituting alternate function implementations on a particular object in JavaScript yields greater flexibility against these concerns.

are much easier to test. They start in the test code uninitialized, allowing you to configure them with entities defined only within the tests, reducing the overall coupling of the test library.

As you can guess from reading the overview of the salient factory seams, only a narrow set of factory characteristics strongly support testability. To best support testability, a factory implementation should not be a singleton and should support flexible initialization and entity registration. Collectively, these constitute a rare combination of features. The infrequency of these features existing together reduces the likelihood of factories being a desirable seam for testing. Here are some recommendations for creating your factories to better support testability.

Because of the testability concerns with singletons in general, you should try to implement your factories as singletons by convention rather than by implementation. Ensure by the way they are constructed that only one instance exists. Many dependency injection frameworks provide mechanisms to support singletons by convention.

A useful factory implementation for testing only needs to support either flexible initialization or dynamic registration. With sufficiently flexible initialization, you can create almost any construction of the entities you wish by changing the initialization parameters. With dynamic registration, you can register the builders or templates to create exactly the right entities. Personally, I prefer dynamic registration over flexible initialization, simply because of the argument presented previously that flexible initialization somewhat defeats the purpose of a factory. That argument does not hold as strongly, however, when flexible initialization supports the creation of more complex networks of entities.

A factory makes a good seam when trying to test a component that uses the factory to generate collaborators. The ability to modify the initialization of generated entities or to register alternate implementations allows you to inject behavior into the software under test through the altered implementations.

While this seems like a clean way to affect the behavior you are testing, it comes at a cost. If you added the factory simply to support testing, a common maneuver for ardent mockists,[12] you are adding code and complexity that itself needs to be tested and maintained.

---

12. Arlo Belshee wrote an insightful blog post about the mocks versus no mocks debate at http://arlobelshee.com/post/the-no-mocks-book that includes an example of creating a factory exclusively for mock injection during testing.

Such a move should have strong justification for the cost. Additionally, factories are typically implementation details; they are a means to an end, not a requirement of the software. As such, using a factory as a seam couples your test to the implementation. Additionally, the collaborators created by the factory are also frequently implementation details that couple the test at least to an interface or template, if not a full-on implementation. Both of these vectors for coupling inhibit the scalability and maintainability of your test regimen. Configuring factories produces looser coupling than using the implementation classes generated by the production factory when injecting behavior, but higher coupling than avoiding the factory entirely.

Factories are useful test seams, especially when testing with a behavioral flavor using mocks or other forms of test double. You should approach the additional coupling and complexity that factories can introduce with informed caution, which is why I choose to put them low on the list of seams to exploit.

Logging and Other Facilities of Last Resort

There are times when all reasonable seams fail your purpose. You beat your head against a wall. "How can I test this piece of code?" you scream in frustration. You want to test the code. You *need* to test the code. Your obsession with mastery over the system will not let you quit. Such moments lead to desperate decisions.

First, take a break. Get some fresh air. Go for a walk. Take a nap. Have a smoke, if that is your vice. Check your e-mail. Read a chapter of a good novel. Do whatever you have to do to break the fixation, distract your brain, and get some space. If after all of that you still need to beat the challenge, read on and consider the end of the test-seam rope, but see Figure 12-1.

I hope I have scared you enough to think carefully before using the techniques I am about to present. They are real. They are useful. Let's start by discussing why they should be applied cautiously.

As we saw in Chapters 4 and 5, we want to verify intent over implementation, minimize coupling, prevent tests from interacting with each other, and avoid techniques that inhibit running tests reliably in parallel. The seams we are about to discuss violate all of these principles. Some facilities in our development frameworks exist for developer convenience. Others have broader applicability, but have much looser requirements for whether and where they are used in our code.

Figure 12-1: *Heed this if you consider using the techniques in this section.*

Logging, monitoring, and sometimes security fall into these categories. While few will tell you to avoid logging, you will rarely be told where to place your logging statements, particularly the ones that only support debugging.

These facilities tend to be optional and implementational. They do not exist in the requirements. Their existence and placement are largely discretionary, deriving a high degree of implementation coupling from dependence on specific usage. At the same time, their role as a centrally configurable and available capability gives them a singleton nature that could allow mistaken test interaction in sequential or parallel execution.

Logging is the most common example of the kind of facility we are discussing. Listing 12-15 shows Java code using log4j.[13] In this case, I added the `debug` statement exclusively for testing purposes to verify an intermediate computation. While most developers use the `message` parameter to the `debug` statement as a `String`, the interface only requires it to be an `Object`, so we can freely pass `intermediate`.

Listing 12-15: *Java code using log4j as an explicitly added debugging seam*

```java
public class SUT {
  private static final Logger LOG =
    Logger.getLogger(SUT.class);

  public void testMe() {
    // Bunch of code
    ...
```

---

13. Note that the other Java logging frameworks like `java.util.logging`, sl4j, and logback all have similar functionality. Most modern logging frameworks in other languages follow suit.

```
    Integer intermediate = computeSomething();
    // Important: Keep this for testing purposes!
    LOG.debug(intermediate);
    // Continue with computation
    ...
  }
}
```

So how can we use this as a seam? Most applications configure log4j through a Java properties file or through XML configuration. The log4j framework comes with a large number of useful appenders—the software components that add messages to the message stream—enough to satisfy most applications. Few applications need to write their own appenders or manipulate them programmatically. However, the log4j framework has a complete programmatic API with which it implements the configuration-based features most developers know and love.

Listing 12-16 shows how we can write a custom appender to capture the logged value and verify it after the code is exercised. Even in a simplified form, the example is a bit lengthy. We define the before and after methods to guarantee that we clean up the appender after every test. Otherwise, we would have to use a `try/catch` with `finally`. We also need to cache the appender so that we can remove it and the prior log level so that we can restore it. Once we do that, verification using the appender is as simple as retrieving the cached value.

Listing 12-16: *Testing the code in Listing 12-15 using a custom logging appender*

```
public class SUTTest {
  private ResultCaptureAppender appender;
  private Level oldLevel;

  @Before
  public void configureAppender() {
    appender = new ResultCaptureAppender();
    Logger log = Logger.getLogger(SUT.class);
    log.addAppender(appender);
    oldLevel = log.getLevel();
    log.setLevel(Level.DEBUG);
  }

  @After
  public void removeAppender() {
    Logger log = Logger.getLogger(SUT.class);
    log.removeAppender(appender);
    log.setLevel(oldLevel);
  }
```

```
@Test
public void testTestMe() {
  Integer expectedIntermediate = 17;
  SUT sut = new SUT();

  sut.testMe();

  assertEquals(expectedIntermediate,
    (Integer) appender.getValue());
}

private class ResultCaptureAppender
    extends AppenderSkeleton {
  private Object value;

  @Override
  protected void append(LoggingEvent loggingEvent) {
    value = loggingEvent.getMessage();
  }

  public Object getValue() {
    return value;
  }
}
}
```

However, the code makes some simplifying assumptions that are not very practical. For one, it assumes that our instrumentation is the last logging statement in the testMe() method. Another logging statement after the one shown would overwrite our cached intermediate value. We could compensate by storing all of the logged objects, even storing their call stacks. If this is a testing mechanism we want to reuse it may be worth it, but we need to recognize that we're building complex testing-support infrastructure that may itself need tests to ensure continued correctness.

The implementation of the appender also chooses to leave issues of casting the type of the message to the caller. This makes the appender general purpose but clutters the tests themselves. Shifting the casting to the appender code runs the risk of throwing bad cast exceptions. We can avoid the exception by testing for types in the appender, but that also increases the complexity of our test instrumentation. Regardless of where the casting or type checking is done, we have coupled our test code to the internal data representation of the intermediate result.

Additional maintenance concerns suggest that we should avoid this technique. We dutifully commented the logging statement to help preserve its presence. How do we guarantee that future maintainers remove the comment if they come up with a better way to test the code? Earlier we discussed what would happen if another logging statement were added after the crucial one. No form of comment would provide a very apparent deterrent to that kind of change. The test failure would highlight it if we were lucky enough to have distinct data in the next log statement. Either way, it would require additional logic to hone in on exactly the logging usage we care about for the test, and additional tests using the technique would complicate things further.

Despite all of the fragility and shortcomings of the technique, there are times when it is the best way to test. Chapter 13 shows an example of using an appender to reproduce a threading race condition in a situation that was otherwise unreachable.

Chapter 13

Parallelism

This chapter introduces techniques to tackle one of the harder testing problems: deterministically reproducing multithreading race conditions. Unlike most of the other techniques presented in this book, the ones in this chapter are less likely to be used in a test-driven development scenario. Race conditions typically show up as bugs, not as behaviors that we predict during development or that we use to derive coverage. However, race-condition bugs can be some of the most frustrating for users, developers, and support people alike. Reproducing these bugs to ensure that they are fixed and stay fixed provides a significant advance in confidence for our software processes and systems. These techniques also apply quite well to system and integration tests, although every defect can be isolated to one or more units for unit-testing purposes.

Most contemporary platforms support threading either explicitly or implicitly. For example, Java was designed for threading and has a strong set of concurrent programming libraries. The Java threading and libraries were not designed from scratch or in a vacuum, however. For example, many features in the `java.util.concurrent` package introduced in Java 5 are based on Doug Lea's research that inspired the RogueWave Threads.h++ libraries for C++ in the 90s.

JavaScript, in contrast, supports threads only indirectly. Operations that initiate socket communications like jQuery's `ajax()` method run the I/O request on a different thread. Also, use of the JavaScript `window .setTimeout()` API invokes a thread in the background. Raw JavaScript addresses the issue through callbacks in asynchronous methods. jQuery improves this with the `Deferred()` implementation.

The principles here will apply to a number of threading environments in different languages and platforms with some level of interpretation in the details.

A Brief Introduction to Threads and Race Conditions

Before we dive into how to test parallel code, let's take a brief tour through the history of parallel programming[1] and the anatomy of a race condition.

Some History

At the dawn of the Computing Age, software ran one instruction at a time. Early operating systems added some level of parallelism, but user-written programs still executed one at a time, only taking a break so that the operating system could function. At first, that break only occurred when the program allowed it, known as **cooperative multitasking**. But this wasn't enough, so the concept was extended to run multiple user programs in much the same way, encapsulated in the concept of a **process**. Processes were segregated into different address spaces and executed in parallel by orchestration of the operating system through a mechanism called **preemptive multitasking**. Each process had its own dedicated memory and other resources. They used a wide number of tricks and new facilities to coordinate with each other, collectively called Inter-Process Communications (IPC) mechanisms.

Eventually, we needed more out of our computers. The overhead of a whole process just to run some activities in parallel and the complexity of IPC mechanisms often just to share some simple data structures motivated the invention of threads. **Threads** execute separately within the same process and share the same memory and data structures. Threads do not share everything, though. Each thread maintains its own execution context, which consists of a limited amount of stack memory and its own instruction path.

---

1. Consider this section a condensed and idealized history. Like most advances in knowledge and practice, the reality is not as linear or logical as presented here. For more detail on threads, Java concurrency libraries, principles of atomicity and immutability, and more, I highly recommend *Java Concurrency in Practice* [JCIP].

Race Conditions

Threads bring us a higher likelihood of bugs because they can access shared data without explicit coordination, whereas IPC mechanisms required significant forethought to apply. In fact, the complexity of writing code that behaves properly in threads warrants its own term. Code is **thread-safe** if it guarantees correctness when running in multiple threads simultaneously.

Most threading bugs are **race conditions**. Generally speaking, race conditions occur when data writes are not properly coordinated. There are three types of race conditions based on the conflicting operation and its order: write-read, read-write, and write-write.

If asynchronous operations that have ordering dependencies are not properly coordinated, you have a **write-read** race condition. The value should be generated or written before it is consumed or read. Bugs in this case occur in the code that coordinates the computations. Listing 13-1 shows this kind of situation in JavaScript. The jQuery `$.get()` asynchronously fetches data from the given URL then runs the supplied callback. In this case, it is nearly certain that it will not finish before `build_menu()` is called, and `menu` will be passed to the menu builder without being initialized.

Listing 13-1: *A write-read race condition in JavaScript*

```
var menu;
$.get('/menu').done(function(response) {
  menu = response;
});


build_menu(menu);
```

A **read-write**, also known as a **test-then-set**, race condition occurs when code uses a value to make a decision about how that value will be changed without ensuring the two operations happen atomically. Let's look at a simple example, a dysfunctional resource initializer implementation (see Listing 13-2).

Listing 13-2: *A simple dysfunctional resource initialization method*

```
1 public Resource initializeResource() {
2   if (resource == null) {
3     resource = new Resource();
4   }
5   return resource;
6 }
```

The race condition occurs between lines 2 and 3. Consider the following sequence of events.

- Thread A executes line 2 and determines that `resource` is `null`.
- The operating system suspends Thread A and resumes Thread B.
- Thread B executes line 2 and determines that `resource` is `null`.
- Thread B executes lines 3–5, allocating an instance of `Resource` and returning it to the caller.
- The operating system suspends Thread B and resumes Thread A.
- Thread A executes lines 3–5, allocating a different instance of `Resource` and returning it to the caller.
- At some later point in time, Thread B calls `initializeResource()` again, `resource` is not `null`, and the method returns a different instance than on the previous invocation.

What happened to the first instance of `Resource`, the one allocated by Thread B? It depends on your language. In Java, it is garbage collected once Thread B's use of it has finished. In C++, it is most likely a memory leak unless you are using some form of thread-safe smart pointers,[2] since Thread B has no reason to know it should free it. Regardless of what happens to the memory, you have now created two resources when you meant to create one.

This demonstrates one of the simplest examples of a *critical section*, a section of code that must be accessed by only one thread at a time to behave correctly. In some machine architectures, this can even occur at the machine- or byte-code level when the low-level instructions generated by the compiler effectively modify a value separately from its final storage, as you might get during a self-assignment operation (e.g., `m += n`).

Write-write race conditions occur less frequently in higher-level languages. Instruction-level write-write races occur more frequently, but as a participant in one of the other races at a higher level. Listing 13-3 shows an example of a write-write race condition that may occur if executed in multiple threads. Suppose you have a queue of items waiting to be processed. Previously, you processed it serially but parallelized it for better throughput. Your code assumes that the last item in the queue should be the last processed. However, once you parallelize the item processing, the second to last item could take longer and finish after the last item, recording the wrong item as the last processed.

---

2. Note that not all smart pointer implementations are thread-safe. Be careful!

Listing 13-3: *A write-write race condition under certain assumptions. If the threads are processing a queue, for example, and the intent is for the last in the queue to be recorded as the last processed, this may not behave as desired.*

```
public void recordLastProcessed(Item item) {
  lastProcessed = item;
}
```

Deadlocks

A **deadlock** occurs when two or more threads stop execution waiting on each other or a shared resource. While race conditions happen generally through a deficiency of locking, deadlocks occur through incorrect or overzealous locking. Listing 13-4 shows two methods that are destined to eventually deadlock.

Listing 13-4: *Two methods likely to deadlock if running on the same object in different threads at the same time*

```
public class ClassA {
  private ClassB that;

  public void doSomething() {
    synchronized(this) {
      synchronized(that) {
        // Do the work
      }
    }
  }

  public void doSomethingElse() {
    synchronized(that) {
      synchronized(this) {
        // Do other work
      }
    }
  }
}
```

Note the opposite orders in which the two methods acquire the locks. What happens if doSomething() acquires the lock on the object, and doSomethingElse() acquires the lock on that before doSomething() can? Both will wait for what the other has and neither will continue. Generally, locking should happen in the same order in all uses—a concept known as **hierarchical locking**—in order to be correct. The switch in order here is a concurrency code smell.

A Strategy for Race Condition Reproduction

Before we get into the specific techniques for reproducing race conditions, let's establish an overall strategy to guide how we approach the problem. Reproducing race conditions requires being able to carefully orchestrate the sequence of events in the critical section, preferably in a way that will not change when we fix the race condition. Understanding the exact nature of the race condition lets us understand the boundaries of the critical section and therefore the scope of our possible control of the execution. We are looking for the seams within the critical section.

In Listing 13-2, our race condition is bounded by testing for the null-ness of `resource` at line 2 and the assignment to `resource` on line 3. There isn't much happening between those two lines, is there? Not really, but understanding the sequence of evaluation gives us more insight and opportunity.

Looking more closely at line 3, we see that a constructor is invoked and that the operator precedence guarantees that the constructor invocation occurs before the variable assignment. This is a seam. Depending on what happens within that constructor, we may have any number of seams to exploit. More complex situations are often rich with seams. Additionally, the underlying threading and execution implementation may offer seams that are not explicitly indicated by a surface inspection of the code.

What do we do with these seams when we find them? We use them to explicitly trigger or simulate the thread suspension that may occur naturally during execution. We will use a collection of techniques to essentially stop a thread until some other execution sequence has completed so that we may then resume the thread to duplicate the race condition behavior.

Let's generalize the approach first. I will outline an analytical approach to diagnosing race conditions. It takes some time to build the experience and the right perspective to be able to pick them out very easily, and you will need familiarity with the synchronization APIs in your environment, but hopefully this will get you on the right path.

1. Identify your race condition.

   - Determine that you may have a race condition.

     Sometimes you will suspect a race because of data corruption. Sometimes you will see unexpected failures that only occur sporadically, such as the exceptions generated in the logging example later in this chapter. Other times you will see things seem to happen in the wrong order. Once in a while, some portion of the application will freeze. Any or all of these could show up. The key is that the erroneous behavior will happen sporadically, often correlated more strongly with particular types of load, or in a way that is very environment specific, such as only on a slower or faster CPU, browser, or network connection. If you can statistically characterize the occurrence of the problem, keep that data as a baseline.

- Make sure the code works correctly in the single-threaded case, if appropriate.

  You will feel really frustrated by spending a lot of time chasing a race condition if it is simply a bug in the algorithm. Occasionally, you will run into code in which the synchronization is so integral to the behavior that correctness verification is difficult. Refactor so that you can verify single-threaded correctness before you go further.

- Create a hypothesis for the nature of the interaction.

  Race conditions are sequencing issues. When the problem involves data corruption, then the sequence of data modification needs fixing. Strange behavior simply involves order of operations. Often the hypothesis requires a fairly deep understanding of the fundamentals of the system, such as how multitasking and timeslicing work, how locks apply in your runtime environment, or how asynchronous callbacks are processed. Formulate a plausible concept of the problem.

- Identify the critical section(s) responsible for the hypothesis.

  This step identifies the code, not just the concept. For data issues, look for places where the code reads and writes the data in separate synchronization scopes. Be aware of whether data structures are thread-safe and what thread-safe guarantees they make. For both data and behavioral issues, look for asynchronous events that have unenforced dependencies on order. For freezes, look for overzealous synchronization, particularly in areas that manage multiple locks and unlock them in an order different from the reverse of the order in which they are locked. Also, look for circular dependencies in synchronized areas.

2. Reproduce the race condition.

   - Validate the hypothesis.

     Once in awhile, you can jump directly to code-based tests and can skip this step. Most of the time, this step involves the debugger.

Pause and run the thread or threads, potentially modifying the data involved. Once you have the recipe for the race, you can proceed. If you cannot duplicate the race in the debugger, either find another critical section or formulate a new hypothesis.

- Identify the seams in the critical section.

  You can apply variations on most of the techniques from the prior chapters of this book to force race conditions. The details of those applications fill the rest of this chapter. You can use almost any seam that allows you to inject a test double. Additionally, you should consider any place that allows you to interact with the locks on the critical section either directly or indirectly. A good example of a nonobvious but available lock in Java is the monitor that is available on all objects through the `wait`/`notify` APIs.

- Choose the right seam.

  From the seams you have identified, eliminate any that you think will disappear when you fix the race condition. You probably have an idea of the fix from your time validating the hypothesis. If the fix will alter a seam, then use of that seam will not result in a test that can validate the fix.

- Exploit the seam to inject synchronization.

  When you validated the hypothesis, you stepped through the code in the debugger to reproduce the race. Now that you have chosen a seam to exploit, use it to programmatically reproduce the sequence of control you developed in the debugger. Write the test to perform that sequence and to assert that the expected outcome does not happen. For deadlocks, a timeout value on the test handles failure nicely. For example, the JUnit `@Test` annotation takes an optional `timeout` parameter.

3. Fix the race condition.

   Now that you have reproduced the race in your test, the test should pass once you fix it.

4. Monitor the results.

   In the first step, I suggested you should characterize the occurrence of the race condition. Unfortunately, you may have found, duplicated, and fixed a race condition different from the one you were trying to find. Ultimately, the proof that you have fixed it is that it occurs less or not at all, but the sporadic nature of race conditions makes that only verifiable through ongoing monitoring. Notice also that I wrote "occurs less." It is possible that there were multiple causes for similar symptoms, and you only found one.

Test the Thread Task Directly

Object-oriented threading libraries generally separate the modeling of a thread from the modeling of the task that the thread runs. Usually, there are also convenience facilities to just use the thread model directly rather than explicitly creating separate instances for each. From its inception, Java has had a `Thread` class and has represented the task with the `Runnable` interface. A `Thread` is a `Runnable`, and its default implementation runs itself as its task.

Shortcomings in this design[3] motivated the addition of the `java.util.concurrent` packages to Java 5. In addition to a broad range of new synchronization facilities, it added `Executor` as the model of execution and `Callable` as the model for the task. The new packages use and support the older thread-related classes out of both convenience and necessity.[4]

Both `Runnable` and `Callable` are defined as interfaces, which helps us untangle some of the testing issues. As interfaces, they represent the methods necessary to execute on a thread, not the actual work done on the thread. This tells us that a task incorporates two distinct purposes, which we may test separately as appropriate. The first is the ability to execute on a thread. The second is the functionality that will be executed on that thread. Examining the task functionality, we will usually see that there is nothing in the task that requires that it be executed on a separate thread.

---

3. Among others, the mechanism to communicate exceptions out of your `Runnable` was awkward and sometimes buggy, and there was no formalization of a return value from the task.

4. `Executor` is not really a replacement for `Thread`; rather, it is an abstraction of a wrapper around `Thread`. While `Callable` is an improvement and replacement for `Runnable`, there are a number of convenience constructors and methods that take a `Runnable` to ease the transition to the newer library. There are also a large number of Java libraries that expect a `Runnable` and were designed before `Callable` existed.

Wait a minute! Why wouldn't a thread task need a separate thread? The nature of many multithreaded algorithms is to segregate most or all of the data such that there is no need to synchronize the access. The synchronization occurs when the data results are joined together. You have to wait for the results anyway. Joining finished results while waiting for others to come in speeds up the computation. This is the essence of MapReduce[5] frameworks and other parallel data partitioning schemes. This means that many tasks do not require any synchronization and can be tested for their computational purpose directly!

So how does this affect our design for testability? First, it suggests that we should ensure that our task is encapsulated in its own testable unit. While it is convenient to implement the task as simply an extension of a `Thread`, we establish a separation of concerns that better supports testability by encapsulating the task in its own class. Second, it is common to use inner classes and anonymous inner classes as the tasks. This usage often hides the details of the task from outsiders who may not need to know them, but it also hides the task from tests. Our tasks are more accessible to tests and therefore more testable if they are modeled as named classes rather than hidden or anonymous ones.

This same principle applies in procedural languages, by the way. For example, the thread library Apple provides for threading on OS X and iOS is distinctly procedural, requiring either function pointers or Objective-C blocks[6] as the task definition. Although it can be convenient to define the tasks inline in this manner, it can make the overall code much harder to unit test.

Let's look at a brief example of refactoring to a separate `Runnable` in Listing 13-5.

Listing 13-5: *Implementing a parallel computation directly as a `Thread`*

```
public void parallelCompute() {
  Thread thread = new Thread() {
    public void run() {
      Result result = computeResult();
      storeResult(result);
    }
    private Result computeResult() {
      ...
```

---

5. See the original Google Research paper on MapReduce at http://research.google.com/archive/mapreduce.html.

6. The Objective-C implementation of closures. The closest analogy of this in Java prior to Java 8 lambdas is anonymous inner classes.

```
  }
  private void storeResult(Result result) {
     ...
  }
};
thread.start();
// Do some things while the thread runs
thread.join();
}
```

Separating the `Runnable` from the `Thread` to a named inner class gives us the code in Listing 13-6.

Listing 13-6: *Refactoring Listing 13-5 to extract the computation into a* `Runnable`

```
public void parallelCompute() {
  Thread thread = new Thread(new ComputeRunnable());
  thread.start();
  // Do some things while the thread runs
  thread.join();
}

private class ComputeRunnable implements Runnable {
  public void run() {
    Result result = computeResult();
    storeResult(result);
  }
  private Result computeResult() {
    ...
  }
  private void storeResult(Result result) {
    ...
  }
}
```

There may be minor refactoring around the storage of `result`, depending on how that is implemented, but the named class provides more options to encapsulate the property as well. Note that even for this skeletal task, factoring out the anonymous inner class greatly improves the readability of the `parallelCompute()` method.

It is a trivial refactoring to extract the named inner class `ComputeRunnable` to a separate class file. From there we can use our other established techniques to test the actual functionality of the class.

But we made a significant assumption here that we said is often but not always true: that the task does not really require thread synchronization to do its job. The remainder of the chapter will introduce techniques for those scenarios.

Synchronize through Common Lock

Existing explicit synchronization gives us one of the easiest seams to exploit. The most common form occurs when the code under test has a critical section that uses another class that is already thread-safe. In such cases, you can use the synchronization in the other class to suspend within the critical section. Consider the code in Listing 13-7.

Listing 13-7: *An example for discussion on common lock synchronization*

```
public final class HostInfoService { // Singleton
  private static HostInfoService instance;
  private HostInfoService() {
    ...
  }

  public static synchronized HostInfoService getInstance() {
    if (instance == null ) {
      instance = new HostInfoService();
    }
    return instance;
  }

  public HostInfo getHostInfo(String hostname) {
    HostInfo hostInfo = new HostInfo();
    ...
    return hostInfo;
  }

public class HostCache {
  private Map<String, HostInfo> hostInfoCache;

  public HostInfo getHostInfo(String hostname) {
    HostInfo info = hostInfoCache.get(hostname);
    if (info == null) {
      info = HostInfoService.getInstance()
          .getHostInfo(hostname);
      hostInfoCache.put(hostname, info);
    }
    return info;
  }
}
```

First of all, where is the race condition? Introspecting on the intent of `HostCache`, this kind of functionality is typically designed to be a singleton instance, even if it is not implemented as a Singleton pattern.

This means that the application will ensure that there is one and only one of these, at least within some shared scope. As a result, the `hostInfoCache` map is a shared data structure, even though it is not static. In Java, `Map<K,V>` is an interface defining a standard key-value storage interface. I have not shown the implementation actually allocated because the implementation type and its synchronization are not the source of our race condition.[7] It also is not the seam we will exploit for our example, although it should be seen as a viable alternative.

Assuming that shared scope involves multiple threads, as is often the case in modern networked applications, the `getHostInfo()` method has a race condition similar to that in our pseudo-singleton from the introduction but a little bit broader.

Assuming the map implementation itself is thread-safe, the start of our critical section is the initial assignment to `info`, where the value obtained from the map is stored locally. From that point until the new value is stored defines the extent of our critical section. The value stored for the key can change between these two points on a different thread and give us two different cached `HostInfo`s for the same key.

So what seams do we have in the critical section? There are three that are immediately apparent by nature of the method calls involved, as follows.

1. `HostInfoService.getInstance()`
2. `HostInfoService.getHostInfo()`
3. `Map.put()`

For this example, we will use the first one, `HostInfoService.get-Instance()`. Our makeshift implementation of `getHostInfo()` is not a very appealing seam, although a more realistic implementation could provide one. `Map.put()` could be difficult to use because we have only exposed the interface, not the implementation, and we are not in control of that code. Keep that thought in mind while we look at the test we would write to reproduce the race condition.

First, let's define a `Callable` to encapsulate the usage that will reproduce the race condition (Listing 13-8). We will create this as a private inner class of our test class.

---

7. Assuming we are using a thread-safe `Map` implementation. `HashMap` (http://docs.oracle.com/javase/6/docs/api/java/util/HashMap.html), perhaps the most commonly used `Map` implementation, is not thread-safe.

Listing 13-8: *A* `Callable` *to help reproduce the race condition in Listing 13-7*

```java
private class GetHostInfoRaceTask

    implements Callable<HostInfo> {
  private final HostCache cache;
  private final String hostname;
  public GetHostInfoRaceTask(HostCache cache,
      String hostname) {
    this.cache = cache;
    this.hostname = hostname;
  }

  @Override
  public HostInfo call() throws Exception {
    return cache.getHostInfo(hostname);
  }
}
```

Passing the `HostCache` into the constructor supports the intended singleton usage of the cache. The `hostname` parameter supports defining the same lookup key for each thread, which is a necessary characteristic for the race condition.

Now that we have our task, the test method to reproduce the race condition is shown in Listing 13-9.

Listing 13-9: *A test to reproduce the race condition in Listing 13-7*

```java
@Test
public void testGetHostInfo_Race()
    throws InterruptedException, ExecutionException {
  HostCache cache = new HostCache();
  String testHost = "katana";
  FutureTask<HostInfo> task1 =
    new FutureTask<HostInfo>(
        new GetHostInfoRaceTask(cache, testHost)
    );
  FutureTask<HostInfo> task2 =
    new FutureTask<HostInfo>(
        new GetHostInfoRaceTask(cache, testHost)
    );

  Thread thread1 = new Thread(task1);
  Thread thread2 = new Thread(task2);

  thread1.start();
  thread2.start();
  HostInfo result1 = task1.get();
  HostInfo result2 = task2.get();
```

```
    Assert.assertNotNull(result1);
    Assert.assertNotNull(result2);
    Assert.assertSame(result1, result2);
}
```

In the pattern of the Four-Phase Test, everything before we start the threads sets up the fixture, starting the threads and obtaining the results from the futures exercises the SUT, the assertions verify the results, and we rely on Garbage-Collected Teardown. We also choose to declare exceptions in the `throws` clause to keep our test as simple as possible. If you run this test several times, it should fail a significant percentage of the runs, always at the `assertSame()` assertion.

We now have a unit test that sporadically fails. However, statistics are not good enough for what we want. It may be tolerable to rely on statistics when tests fail as much as 25–50% of the time like this one. When subtler race conditions manifest in failure rates below 1%, and the overall test bed takes even a moderate time to run—say five minutes—it would take on average over four hours[8] to start to have reasonable confidence of a fix. Let's make the race condition predictable.

Looking at the implementation of the `getInstance()` method, we see that the method is `synchronized`. The method could have also used explicit synchronization on a specific static object instead, and many would say that that is better practice, but for our purposes it does not matter, so we use the briefer formulation.

In Java, a synchronized method synchronizes on its object instance. But this is a static synchronized method, so it synchronizes on its class object. In either case, the object acts as a **monitor** to control exclusive execution to all similarly synchronized methods. The synchronization primitives themselves are built into the `Object` class from which every Java class derives.

We will use this fact about Java synchronization to trap our test threads in the middle of the critical section, ensuring that they trigger the race condition failure mode. How can we ensure that the monitor for the `HostInfoService` is taken when the threads get to it? Let's enclose the two calls to `Thread.start()` in a synchronized block.

---

8. Five minutes times 100 gives 500 minutes, or just over eight hours. Statistically, there is a 50% probability that we would see the failure in the first four hours or so.

But wait, that only guarantees that the class monitor is locked when the threads are started, not that it will be locked when they arrive at the call to the `getInstance()` method. We have a race condition in our test setup! We can remedy this easily. I anticipated this and chose to use explicit `Thread` instances to run the tasks rather than using something like a `ThreadPoolExecutor`, as might be suggested by the use of `Callable`. While the executor does a nice job of encapsulating and managing the threads for production purposes, we want to have a little more insight and control than that encapsulation allows.

Java has a well-defined state machine for a thread's life cycle. Specifically, when a Java thread is waiting on a monitor, it enters the `Thread.State.BLOCKED` state until it is released. It would be bad style to create a busy wait for this state in production code, but our test is simple and deterministic. The two lines to start the thread now become part of the fixture setup and look like Listing 13-10 (added lines in bold type).

Listing 13-10: *Ensuring that test threads are blocked before testing. The bold-faced lines are added around the corresponding lines from Listing 13-9.*

```
synchronized (HostInfoService.class) {
  thread1.start();
  while (thread1.getState() != Thread.State.BLOCKED) { }
  thread2.start();
  while (thread2.getState() != Thread.State.BLOCKED) { }
}
```

By the time our test leaves the `synchronized` block, both of our threads are waiting on the `HostInfoService.class` monitor in the middle of the critical section. One of the threads will obtain the lock and continue. The other will wait until the lock is released. Either way, we have deterministically reproduced the race condition. The test now fails 100% of the time in its original implementation without any changes to the code under test.

We can now easily fix the race condition in any of several ways. Opting for the easiest for demonstration purposes, let's just add `synchronized` to the method definition for `HostCache.get-HostInfo()` so that it looks like

```
public synchronized HostInfo getHostInfo(String hostname) {
```

You could refine the scope a little by putting an explicit `synchronized` block only around the critical section, leaving the return outside and requiring `info` to be defined, but not assigned, before the block.

Depending on the overall synchronization needs of the class, the block could synchronize on `this` or on a special lock object allocated just to protect this critical section.

Although the specifics of `Object` monitors are very Java-centric, similar mechanisms exist in all thread-synchronization libraries. Not all are as tightly integrated to the object model, but monitors, mutexes, and critical sections are some of the universal building blocks of thread programming.

As a final note, more complicated locking schemes may require a higher level of ingenuity. For example, we implemented a busy wait in the test until the thread was blocked. How do we know it was blocked at the point at which we thought it was? Does it matter? The short answers are, "We don't" and "Maybe."

In our simple example, it made our test deterministically fail, and inspection tells us that there is no other hypothesis to explain it. We could also put the test in the debugger and verify that the threads are blocked at the expected location before leaving the `synchronized` block. If the code does not change—a very poor assumption to make about any production code—then simply making the test reproducible should be sufficient evidence. However, for code maintenance purposes, we should know that it is behaving the way we designed it to behave, but there is no programmatic way to assert that.

Synchronize through Injection

Synchronizing through a common lock works well as long as the common lock exists and is accessible. But what do you do when the lock is not available, or the locks that are available are in the wrong places? You create your own!

Chapter 12 looked at the various ways you can use injection points as seams. Whether through dependency injection frameworks, callbacks, registries, or logging and monitoring frameworks, the ability to inject a test double allows you to also inject synchronization.

Example: Injecting Synchronization through Logging

Although I quite melodramatically warned against exploiting logging frameworks for testing, some race conditions require their use. Let's look at a real-life example I encountered.

Consider the code in Listing 13-11. At first blush, it may appear that this code is thread-safe. Java guarantees that the individual operations of the `Vector` class are thread-safe. The retrieval of the first element and its removal are in a `synchronized` block. However, small though it may be, the time between the test for whether `logRecords` is empty in the `while` condition and the `synchronized` block in which that test is acted on represents a classic check-and-modify race condition. When this method in invoked in high volumes, the call to `logRecords.firstElement()` occasionally throws a `NoSuchElementException`, indicating that the container is empty.

Listing 13-11: *An example of a race condition with a logging seam*

```
private static final Logger =
  Logger.getLogger(AuditTrail.class);
private final Vector<AuditRecord> logRecords =
  new Vector<AuditRecord>();

public void postFlush(...) {
  ...
  while (!logRecords.isEmpty()) {
    log.debug("Processing log record");
    AuditRecord logRecord;
    synchronized (logRecords) {
      logRecord = logRecords.firstElement();
      logRecords.remove(logRecord);
    }
    // Process the record
    ...
  }
}
```

Fortunately, the original code author included a debugging statement in the loop. Listing 13-12 shows an `Appender` that we can use to exploit the seam. It simply waits, using itself as the monitor whenever a message is appended. If there were more than one log statement, or we wanted the lock to engage conditionally, we could create a more sophisticated implementation.

Listing 13-12: *A log4j `Appender` implementation for thread-synchronization control*

```
class SynchronizationAppender extends AppenderSkeleton {
  @Override
  protected void append(LoggingEvent loggingEvent) {
    try {
      this.wait();
```

```
  } catch (InterruptedException e) {
    return;
  }
}
... // Other required overrides
}
```

Listing 13-13[9] shows how the `Appender` from Listing 13-12 can be used to reproduce the race condition and eventually verify our fix. It runs the software under test on a separate thread after configuring log4j to use the custom `Appender`. After ensuring that the thread gets into the waiting state induced by the log statement, it removes the queued record and releases the thread. The thread was executed using a `Callable`, whose `Future` object is used to determine whether the `NoSuchElementException` is thrown. The exception indicates test failure.

Listing 13-13: *Using the `Appender` from Listing 13-12 to force the race condition in Listing 13-11*

```
@Test
public void testPostFlush_EmptyRace()
        throws InterruptedException, ExecutionException {
    // Set up software under test with one record
    AuditRace sut = new AuditRace();
    sut.addRecord();
    // Set up the thread in which to induce the race
    Callable<Void> raceInducer = new PostFlushCallable(sut);
    FutureTask<Void> raceTask =
      new FutureTask<Void>(raceInducer);
    Thread inducerThread = new Thread(raceTask);
    // Configure log4j for injection
    SynchronizationAppender lock =
      new SynchronizationAppender();
    Logger log = Logger.getLogger(AuditRace.class);
    log.addAppender(lock);
    log.setLevel(Level.DEBUG);

    inducerThread.start();
    while (Thread.State.WAITING != inducerThread.getState());
    // We don't want this failure
    // to look like the race failure
```

---

9. This example was originally used in an article for InformIT magazine. The full code example can be found with the article at http://www.informit.com/articles/article .aspx?p=1882162.

```
    try {
        sut.getLogRecords().remove(0);
    } catch (NoSuchElementException nsee) {
        Assert.fail();
    }
    synchronized (lock) {
        lock.notifyAll();
    }

    raceTask.get();
}
```

I will repeat that this technique requires some caution. The same reasons that programmers typically overlook logging statements as testing seams can also contribute to fragile tests, particularly when forcing race conditions. Casually removing the logging statement used as a seam can lead to unusual test failures. The `try`/`catch` around the removal of the queued record attempts to capture the possibility, but it could still require some careful diagnosis. Similarly, the addition of extra logging statements, in combination with the simple implementation of the `SynchronizationAppender`, could cause the test to hang indefinitely and possibly fail due to timeouts. Conditionally waiting based on the first execution or on the content of the message being logged could address those concerns.

The other important step omitted in this example is the removal of the shared `Appender`. The power of logging frameworks like log4j derives from a central singleton nature that coordinates the logging activity and configuration. The unique instance is a shared resource across all tests, which can cause appender changes to apply to other tests. A more robust implementation would preserve the existing appender structure and restore it at the end of the test.

Use Supervisory Control

Sometimes, when you are testing, you just cannot find a seam. Maybe a class is too well encapsulated. Perhaps the designer of the software under test did not recognize a need to allow the calling code to insert behavioral or monitoring hooks into the software. Maybe the software is already highly synchronized to a point at which it "couldn't possibly have a race condition," at least until the ongoing evolution of the system changes the assumptions under which it was originally thread-safe.

The latter happened in a system I worked with at one time. Imagine a system in which autonomous agents[10] collaborate in a manner governed by a tightly designed state machine to collectively achieve the application goal. In this particular system, agents organized in a way to effectively model cause–effect relationships patiently waited for messages on a blocking queue from their causative predecessors. Life was good, orderly, and well synchronized in the agents' world.

Then we recognized the need for human influence on the process. Suddenly, events could come in sequences that were not anticipated by the state machine because of the inherently asynchronous nature of human interaction. One particularly inventive system tester created a test harness that rapidly and randomly exerted external influence on the system like an angry child at a keyboard. This system test alone generated a multitude of parallelism bugs literally overnight. Given that the system had very high robustness requirements and hundreds of users interacting with it at a time, the test was only a mild exaggeration of anticipated usage.

The challenge occurred because the race condition was found in the interaction between a very simple loop and an off-the-shelf concurrency component, much like the Java code[11] in Listing 13-14.

Listing 13-14: *A race condition in working with thread-safe components*

```java
import java.util.concurrent.BlockingQueue;

class Agent implements Runnable {
  private BlockingQueue<Event> incoming;
  ...
  @Override
  public void run() {
    processEvents();
  }
}
```

---

10. Software components that operate independently with a locally defined set of tasks to collectively effect emergent behaviors. The typical examples of autonomous agents from the natural world are ants, bees, and birds. For example, you can algorithmically define the behavior of a single bird relative to the movements of its nearest birds to effectively and accurately simulate the behavior of the entire flock.

11. You may want to reference the Javadoc for the `BlockingQueue` interface if you are interested in the details. It can be found at http://docs.oracle.com/javase/6/docs/api/java/util/concurrent/BlockingQueue.html.

```
public void processEvents() {
  Event event;
  while (event = incoming.take()) { // Blocks
    processEvent(event);
  }
}

public void addEvent(Event event) {
  incoming.put(event);
}

private void processEvent(Event event) {
  // Do something with the event
  }
}
```

One problem in particular occurred when two of a particular type of event arrived in rapid succession. In the wild, it happened that two of the same event could arrive at effectively the same time, and both of them would be queued. In isolated unit testing, we could never stuff the queue fast enough to recreate the condition.

So where is the seam? We have an almost trivial, very tight loop operating on a black-box data structure supplied by the system. The only apparent seam is a private method that we would rather not expose.[12] At this point, I would encourage you to put down the book for a moment, think about the nature of preemptive multitasking, and see if you can figure out where the invisible seam resides.

The answer is in how the thread itself time slices. The point at which the loop blocks waiting for an event is a well-defined state. Because the thread life cycle in Java is explicit, we know the thread state when the loop is blocking. Java has methods to suspend and resume threads. These methods have been deprecated because in production systems this is a deadlock-prone way to synchronize tasks. However, for our purposes this is ideal and not susceptible to deadlock because of the simple and linear nature of our test. The test to deterministically reproduce the double-event bug might look like Listing 13-15.

---

12. In the real-life system, the equivalent of processEvent() was protected, but the bug occurred in a specific implementation of it that was itself strongly encapsulated and complex enough that it wouldn't have been a good test to try to modify a copy of it.

Listing 13-15: *A test to deterministically reproduce the bug in Listing 13-14*

```java
public class AgentTest {
  @Test
  public void testProcessEvents() {
    Agent sut = new Agent();
    Thread thread = new Thread(sut);
    thread.start();
    while(thread.getState() != Thread.State.BLOCKED) {}
    thread.suspend(); // Freeze the thread
    // Queue up the double event
    sut.addEvent(new ProblematicEvent());
    sut.addEvent(new ProblematicEvent());
    thread.resume(); // Bug triggered!
  }
}
```

By putting the thread into a known state and suspending it, we guarantee that no processing will occur while we set up the aberrant conditions. Of course, this test is missing assertions about the outcome of successful event processing, but you can add that in when you apply this to your own real world situation.

Statistical Verification

The sporadic nature of race conditions sometimes defies strictly deterministic reproduction. However, many factors contribute to the occurrence of race conditions, including load, frequency, transactional volume, and timing. When explicit control eludes you, these factors become your friends.

Statistical verification works best at coarser granularities of testing, such as system and integration tests. It can be applied effectively at lower levels as well, but oftentimes, the exact conditions contributing to the race condition are harder to isolate and reproduce. At times, the integrated system produces interactions and timings that evade our ability to diagnose and reproduce. Additionally, coarser-granularity test beds may have a higher tolerance for the longer run times that can be associated with statistical verification.

There are several forms of statistical verification that can be useful. The simplest, running the test enough times to almost guarantee a failure, leverages the sporadic nature of race conditions. It helps if you have an understanding of the frequency of the failure. If you know a test fails 1% of the time, then running it 100 times gives you a reasonable likelihood of reproducing the failure. Does it give you a guarantee of failure? No. However, the likelihood of inducing a failure asymptotically approaches 100% the more times you run the test. Generally speaking, assuming the conditions are such that the per-run probability of failure, P_f, is constant, the total probability of failure, P_F, over n runs is

$$P_F = 1 - (1 - P_f)^n$$

So with a 1% individual failure rate, it takes 300 iterations for a 95% likelihood of failure and over 450 iterations for a 99% chance, as shown in Figure 13-1.

In many cases, race conditions only occur under concurrent loads. The likelihood of the race condition manifesting relates more to the number of concurrent participants than to the number of times through the code. Correlating failure rates against actor volumes provides a scientific approach to determining concurrent failure loads. This can provide surprising insights when graphed against system metrics (e.g., memory or page faults) or events (e.g., garbage collection, notifications, or logins). A well-instrumented system will give you

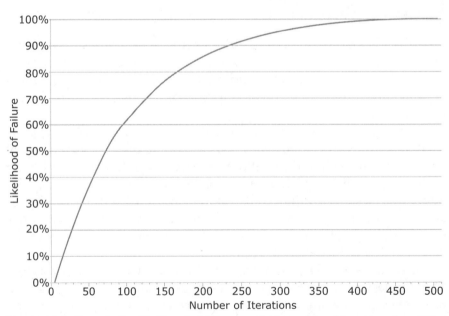

Figure 13-1: *Cumulative likelihood of failure against number of iterations for a 1% individual failure rate*

application-specific usage metrics that you can use for correlation, as well as realistic event sequences that you can replay. In the absence of such analytical data, a trial and error approach can be applied.

The "monkey test" is a useful form of black box exploratory testing for concurrency issues. The name of this form of testing alludes to the Infinite Monkey Theorem, which visualizes a monkey randomly typing at a keyboard. As it pertains to concurrency testing, a framework that randomly injects inputs and signals into a system creates a very effective stress test of that system if run for enough time. In one system I worked on that involved a graph-structured network of autonomous agents (the system discussed earlier in Use Supervisory Control), randomly starting and stopping nodes in the network during operation revealed a wealth of concurrency bugs, including several that could be deterministically reproduced once understood.

Debugger APIs

Think back for a moment to some of your first programming experiences, the ones right after you discovered or were shown how to use the debugger. It changed how you interacted with the software. Instead of inserting print statements only to rip or comment them out later, you could step through, skipping over the parts irrelevant to your investigation and dropping to statement-level or even assembly-level detail to know intimately how your software really operated.

Have you used a debugger that handles multiple threads well? It vastly simplifies the task of controlling the interactions between the threads. You can pause a thread at a break point and walk it and the threads it interacts with through their executions in whatever sequence you wish.

Hmmm. That sounds a lot like what we've been doing with all of the previous techniques. Every instruction then becomes a seam, a place we can insert some level of control to reproduce race conditions, constrained only by the fundamental rules of the underlying machine or virtual machine execution model.

But how do debuggers do that? In short, every execution environment that pretends to multitask—and a few that don't—has APIs for programmatic control of execution. Debuggers are just programs that use an esoteric set of interfaces. In the form in which we typically encounter them, they exercise their exquisite control based on our manually issued commands. Set a break point. Run to a particular line. Watch for a variable to change. With sufficient ingenuity, these same APIs can be used to exploit atomic seams.

Such power comes with a cost. Some debuggers require special privileges to execute, privileges that you may not want to grant to your automated test suite that any developer or tester could modify. Using these APIs often requires a detailed understanding of the underlying execution model, which at a minimum requires a steep and long learning curve on a technology that probably will not be used frequently unless you write compilers or debuggers.

If we jump to a level outside of code, we have more opportunity to leverage this technique. Although it may seem quaint in the age of highly capable, graphical IDEs, the lowly command-line debugger can mitigate the costs of this approach. Many command-line debuggers, including gdb, jdb, and the Perl debugger, are scriptable to varying degrees, allowing their use in automation frameworks.

One application of this technique uses the command-line debugger to set a variable watch that triggers a macro during a Monte Carlo simulation. The variable watch establishes the deviant condition that characterizes the sporadic failure. The commands associated with triggering the watch constitute the output you wish to receive when you've detected the deviant condition. The gdb commands[13] in Listing 13-16 might display the stack trace, then continue execution when the reference count is nonzero at the end of a hypothetical garbage collection in a memory pool.

Listing 13-16: *gdb commands to verify a reference count at the end of a run*

```
break finalize_gc if refs > 0
commands
bt      # Stack trace
cont
end
```

While this is certainly not a complete test-automation or race-reproduction solution, it can be a valuable tool in isolating race conditions and even in characterizing their rates of occurrence. Take, for

---

13. The gdb documentation can be found at http://sourceware.org/gdb/onlinedocs/gdb/Break-Commands.html#Break-Commands.

example, the variation shown in Listing 13-17 on the garbage collection scenario previously covered. The sole purpose of this set of commands is to compute the failure percentage.

Listing 13-17: *Computing failure percentage using the debugger*

```
break gc
commands
set num_gcs = num_gcs + 1
cont
end

break finalize_gc if refs > 0
commands
set num_failures = num_failures + 1
refs = 0
cont
end

break exit
commands
printf "Garbage collection failure rate: %f%%\n", \
  num_failures/num_gcs
cont
end
```

Part III

Worked Examples

Seeing techniques presented in isolation, regardless of whether they are supported by examples, only goes part way toward conveying understanding. You need to see the techniques in action and use them to really achieve mastery. I cannot use the techniques for you. That is your responsibility. However, I can show you how they might be used in realistic scenarios through worked examples.

I have chosen two projects in different languages and testing styles to provide variety of guidance. The first example is a new project in Java executed with a test-driven approach. For the second project, I chose an untested, open-source JavaScript UI component to bring under test.

Both of the examples reside in my GitHub account. I performed both projects as a series of micro-commits so that you can see in detail how they unfolded. Because of the public availability of the gory details, I have chosen to save a few trees and use the printed page to provide a narrative for the projects, interspersed with code excerpts. The narrative is further enhanced with references to the GitHub repositories. Annotations in the in the code like [badd0g5] refer to Git commit hashes. You can find the exact commit by appending it to the commit path for the relevant repository. For example, if the above hash were a commit (which it is not) in my nonexistent "greatsoftware" repository, the URL for the diff would be

```
https://github.com/srvance/greatsoftware/commit/badd0g5
```

and the URL

```
https://github.com/srvance/greatsoftware/tree/badd0g5
```

would show the browsable source tree at that point in the development.

Chapter 14

Test-Driven Java

The first example demonstrates the use of test-driven development to create a new application in Java. I call the project WebRetriever; it is basically a work-alike of a subset of the command-line `curl(1)`[1] command found in most Linux distributions and Mac OS X. If you are not familiar with `curl`, it is a tool for retrieving content over the internet that can be specified as URIs, including authentication, cookie management, and many more features.

The project has the benefit of being relatively small and straightforward, yet ripe for a number of the techniques from the book, in no small part due to its use of the network and, more specifically, the Apache HttpClient[2] library. The repository for this project can be found on GitHub at https://github.com/srvance/QualityCode14 as a series of micro-commits detailing the evolution of the software, missteps and all.

WebRetriever supports the following features, in which command line options refer to the corresponding option in the `curl` documentation.

- Takes options followed by one or more URLs.
- Retrieves content from URLs and writes content to the terminal unless options say otherwise.

---

1. http://curl.haxx.se/docs/manpage.html
2. http://hc.apache.org/httpcomponents-client-ga/index.html

- Supports *only* HTTP, defaulting to GET.
- Assumes HTTP if not specified.
- Supports -O to write the file to the same local name.
  - ○ `curl` applies this option to the *next* URI. You need to put it before every URI if there are multiples you want handled this way.
  - ○ `curl` happily overwrites files if the file exists, including if there are multiple files with the same name in a single invocation.
  - ○ `curl` complains if there is no explicit file name, as in the default index for a site.

I have omitted some practices from this project that I would normally include and endorse. I did not set up static checkers in the Maven build and only relied on the default feedback from my IDE for style and error checking. Ordinarily, I would integrate either Checkstyle, PMD, and FindBugs (all three) or Sonar into the build and configure them for immediate feedback in the IDE. I would normally also use code coverage tools to provide feedback on the thoroughness of my testing. The focus on techniques leads me to omit that here. Finally, I have skipped writing Javadoc for the production code in the interests of brevity and keeping focus on techniques.

Bootstrapping

A purely test-driven project starts with a test. However, creating the repo in GitHub creates a README.md if you want it to be able to clone it. This is a good opportunity to write the spec for the project, or at least the initial spec, so I wrote that first.

Next, I used Maven's archetype generation to set up the structure of the project. I chose an archetype that generated a project for Java-executable JARs, which generated the main class and its test class. As discussed in Chapter 6, I started with the constructor. I did not have an immediate need for attributes, so as the full recipe for bootstrapping the constructor did not apply, I squeezed a simple default construction test [445f41f] between various project setup commits. Test-driving begins in earnest with [0c2d67e].

Notice that I start by testing the construction of an instance and the primary method of interest for the first feature. I do not test the `main()` method. Why is that?

Unless your class has significant static content, it can be almost impossible to test a `main()`. While you could invoke `main()` from a test method as a static method, it generally creates a nonstatic instance of its own class or another to do the work. The best approach keeps the `main` as thin as possible, thinking of it only as the top exception handling layer around the functionality of the program. The simpler it remains, the less you miss by not testing it. You will see the complexity of WebRetriever's `main()` fluctuate a little over the course of the project, but it will eventually settle to a very simple form.

First Functionality

Applying the recipe from Chapter 3, I jumped immediately into the happy path. The purpose of the application is to retrieve content from URLs. The simplest happy path retrieves content from a single URL. I defined the basic `retrieve()` method through its test (Listing 14-1).

Listing 14-1: *Defining a simple `retrieve()` method by using it in its test [0c2d67e]. This "fails" because the method does not exist.*

```
@Test
public void testRetrieve_SingleURI() {
  WebRetriever sut = new WebRetriever();

  String content = sut.retrieve("http://www.example.com");
}
```

For now, in the spirit of YAGNI, the simplest implementation takes the URL and returns the retrieved content as strings, deferring the questions of command-line arguments and output.

Over the next several commits, up to [839e4dc], we evolve the test so that it expresses our full intent and the implementation so that it passes. At this point, the test needs to be strengthened, as it relies only on containment. By most definitions, the test does not qualify as a unit test because it opens a socket to a web page as well. However, in the interest of getting it working first, this represents good progress. I used the Apache HttpClient library to avoid writing the entire protocol myself. After all, test driving does not mean you should reinvent everything.

In the process of manually exploring to ensure that my test data was appropriate, I discovered that the test URL actually uses an HTTP

302 response to redirect to a different host. The HttpClient library handles this transparently to the calling code, a behavior in which WebRetriever operates differently from `curl`. One of the benefits of a goal of creating work-alike software is the availability of the original as your benchmark. I will ignore this difference, although `curl`'s behavior was essential in discovering the redirect.

A few refactoring commits up through [1b49d37] bring us to the first significant testability changes.

Cutting the Cord

When you test-drive, you create the seams that support your testing intent. Recognizing that the `retrieve()` method (Listing 14-2)

- Was a bit long
- Had no ready-made seams with which to sever the network connection for testing
- And performed a wide variety of low-level mechanics in support of its purpose

I decided to simplify and encapsulate it before continuing. Commit [c602d34] was the first application of this principle for WebRetriever.

Listing 14-2: *The working but unwieldy and poorly testable first version of* `WebRetriever.retrieve()`

```
public String retrieve(String URI) throws IOException {
  HttpClient httpClient = new DefaultHttpClient();
  HttpGet httpGet = new HttpGet(URI);
  HttpResponse response = httpClient.execute(httpGet);
  HttpEntity entity = response.getEntity();
  InputStream content = entity.getContent();
  StringWriter writer = new StringWriter();
  IOUtils.copy(content, writer);
  return writer.toString();
}
```

Looking at the method, you can categorize it as setup, execution, and response processing, very much like the first three phases of a test. Unlike a test, you do not need to preserve the boundaries between the phases when you refactor. I chose to extract the retrieval of the response, consisting of set up and execution, as a single method (Listing 14-3).

Listing 14-3: *Refactoring the code from Listing 14-2 to provide a seam, allowing us to avoid the network connection for at least some of our tests [c602d34]*

```
public String retrieve(String URI) throws IOException {
  HttpResponse response = retrieveResponse(URI);
  HttpEntity entity = response.getEntity();
  InputStream content = entity.getContent();
  StringWriter writer = new StringWriter();
  IOUtils.copy(content, writer);
  return writer.toString();
}

protected HttpResponse retrieveResponse(String URI)
    throws IOException {
  HttpClient httpClient = new DefaultHttpClient();
  HttpGet httpGet = new HttpGet(URI);
  return httpClient.execute(httpGet);
}
```

The following commits, through [c1d4b2f], use EasyMock to exploit the seam, although in an ugly and implementation-coupled way. That will be addressed in time. The commits through [b61f107] do some additional refactoring to improve both the test and the code under test in preparation for the next feature.

Moving to Multiples

The commits through [4bdedba] proceed to the handling of multiple URLs to be retrieved. At this point, I only handle direct retrieval with no modifiers, so the easiest approach was to create a new entry point that accepted multiple URLs and looped, invoking the existing `retrieve()` method for each. This required some elaboration of the spec for how multiple bodies of content should be displayed successively.

The driving test for this functionality was written in [5334caa]. This test creates a stub that uses a counter to return different content for each invocation. Different returns help to insulate the test from the accidental appearance of correctness.

Some would object to the use of `StringUtils.join()` both in the test and in the production code. I do not hold this concern. First, I used a different form of the method in each location. Second, as `StringUtils.join()` is a third-party utility that only represents a minor part of the functionality, I do not feel that the correspondence between the test and code implementations is critical.

Before moving on to the next feature, I decided to flesh out the `main` for some manual testing. As much of a fan as I am of unit testing as the foundation for a testing strategy, you need the rest of the strategy. If I were not trying to focus purely on the application of the testing techniques, I might use a BDD tool like Cucumber to create higher-level acceptance tests. For this project, I will just rely on manual testing. Commit [ead7038] fills in an initial implementation of `main()`. The implementation is a little heavier than it should be—something that will need to be addressed as we proceed—but it is adequate for now.

Ghost Protocol

The specification states that WebRetriever should default the protocol, or the *scheme* in the language of the governing RFCs,[3] to HTTP. Some exploration during the newly enabled manual test revealed that this feature was not yet implemented. Being next on the list and proven to be missing, I proceeded to implement this feature.

Dead End

I started by refactoring to create a dependency injection seam [63797de]. The idea was to inject an `HttpClient` mock that would allow me to inspect the resulting argument to its `execute()` method in `retrieve-Response()`. To that end, I elevated the `HttpClient` instance to a class field initialized in the default constructor, which I now needed to make explicit. I then factored out a constructor that took an `HttpClient` instance as an argument and reworked the default constructor to chain to the new one, passing a fresh instance.

In writing the test to exploit the seam, I discovered that many of the methods of `DefaultHttpClient` and `AbstractHttpClient`, including the single-argument version of `execute()` that the code uses, are final, preventing override and therefore obviating the injection approach. Commit [03e0517] removed the new constructor but kept the new version of the default constructor and left the `HttpClient` instance as a field.

---

3. RFC 1630 first defined URLs, URNs, and URIs. Various refinements culminated in RFC 3986 in 2005, which is the current governing specification as of this writing.

Spy Craft

In a way, the wrong turn helped me. Injecting a mock could have been an effective testing technique, but it would also couple the test to the implementation more tightly through the use of an internal type. This is the biggest danger in testing with mocks: the degree of coupling they introduce. [7f74b88] introduces a nicely uncoupled test, shown in Listing 14-4.

Listing 14-4: *An implementation-independent test for the behavior of defaulting the protocol to HTTP*

```
@Test
public void testRetrieveResponse_DomainOnly()
    throws IOException {
  WebRetriever sut = new WebRetriever();

  HttpResponse response =
    sut.retrieveResponse("www.example.com");

  assertThat(response, is(notNullValue()));
}
```

The concept behind the mock approach would have allowed me to inspect the URL passed into the library executing the retrieval. As currently formulated, I pass the URL as a string, which leads to all the challenges of string verification discussed in Chapter 7 except that I do not control the code; it happens inside of `HttpClient`. This led me to consider two points.

1. I would prefer to have a more structured way to inspect the format of the URL.

2. I probably need to create my own seam because `HttpClient` does not support what I need to use its components as test doubles.

The first point led me quickly to consider the `java.net.URI` class for a more structured understanding of the URL. It provides the ability to parse URI strings, and `HttpClient` accepts it as an alternate format for URL arguments.

The `URI` class also suggested how I could create the seam. The `URI` class provides more structure and `HttpClient` accepts it, but the URLs still come in from the command-line arguments as strings. This suggests the need for a translation layer, an ideal place for a seam! Changing `retrieveResponse()` to convert the string URL to a `URI` to give to the `HttpGet` constructor [228d5c7] lets us refactor an overload of `retrieveResponse()` that takes a `URI` argument (Listing 14-5).

Listing 14-5: *The refactored `retrieveResponse()` gives us a seam to exploit.*

```
protected HttpResponse retrieveResponse(String URI)
    throws IOException, URISyntaxException {
  URI uri = new URI(URI);
  return retrieveResponse(uri);
}

protected HttpResponse retrieveResponse(URI uri)
    throws IOException {
  HttpGet httpGet = new HttpGet(uri);
  return httpClient.execute(httpGet);
}
```

Commit [05e5c03] creates a spy to capture the ultimate `URI` that is used to construct an `HttpGet` and uses it to verify that it handles the scheme according to spec. The resulting test and spy are shown in Listing 14-6.

Listing 14-6: *Modifying the test from Listing 14-4 to create a spy exploiting the seam introduced in Listing 14-5*

```
@Test
public void testRetrieveResponse_DomainOnly()
    throws IOException, URISyntaxException {
  WebRetrieverURISpy sut = new WebRetrieverURISpy();

  sut.retrieveResponse("www.example.com");

  URI actualURI = sut.getSuppliedURI();
  assertThat(actualURI.getHost(),
    is(equalTo("www.example.com")));
  assertThat(actualURI.getScheme(), is(equalTo("http")));
}

private class WebRetrieverURISpy extends WebRetriever {
  URI suppliedURI;

  @Override
  protected HttpResponse retrieveResponse(URI uri)
      throws IOException {
    this.suppliedURI = uri;
    return createMockResponse("");
  }
```

```
public URI getSuppliedURI() {
  return suppliedURI;
}
}
```

The spy inserts itself in the middle and captures the URI for later inspection, invoking the behavior of the overridden method so that the actual behavior proceeds unhindered. This allows the test to obtain the structured representation of the URI for the assertions. The test captures the deficiency in the code. I fixed it in the same commit. The next few commits (up to [897bfab]) do some refactoring, add a test to assure that the existing supported behavior still works, and enforce that the *only* supported scheme is HTTP.

Exercising Options

For the next feature, I started supporting options. Perhaps the most useful option writes the retrieved content to a file, although you could always redirect the output without it. I started work on the "-O" option by updating the specification to detail curl's behavior in [bb7347e].

The path to support this option meanders a bit. Admittedly, I did not start with a complete or clean concept of how the feature would be implemented. Rather, I started with an idea of how the arguments might be processed but only a clear understanding that the output handling might be tricky to test properly. I decided to show the messiness and the associated variations of testing rather than doing exploratory spikes and then reverting them to take a clean route. I hope the result is more informative that way.

I used the multiple URL overload of retrieve() to write the test [d451e31] as if it were designed to handle options. The initial test did not completely express the overall intent. Rather, it simply stated that given two arguments, an option and a URL, only one retrieval should occur. I accomplished this by using an anonymous inner class to create a mock, but without a mocking framework. The mock counted the calls to the single URI version of retrieve() and asserted inline that it was only called once. I missed a couple of details on the first pass and finally got the failure I expected in [4102ad1].

Commit [3422f2e] added test and logic to explicitly indicate the request for a write to a file. A little bit of back and forth—fortunately more forth than back—teased out the concept of an emit() method to handle the output [b994220], although the idea was far from fully baked.

The realization that I had scattered necessary state for output across several levels of method calls and abstractions led me to embark on a series of refactorings, starting with [87ae64d]. This included eliminating the previously created spy by testing `rectifyURI()` directly. Most notably, though, I created the concept of a `Target`, first as a nested class and eventually as a full top-level class [46978e9] with its own set of tests [dde0a09]. `Target` at first became the repository for the data associated with a retrieval, but it evolved to be the central entity for the functionality as well [13df657].

Some of the intermediate stages were pretty ugly, especially in the tests. Once it became clear that most of the functionality belonged in `Target`, I migrated the easy functionality, but other methods were trickier. The methods that had been overridden resisted movement, testimony to the dangers of coupling tests to implementation. In some cases, I had to comment out overrides before IntelliJ would allow me to move a method. Then I would uncomment them and move and adjust them to the new context. Ultimately, I achieved a cleaner set of code with which to finish the output flag feature.

After a few cleanup commits, I refactored the `extractContent-FromResponse()` method in a way that prepared to switch entirely over to a stream-based approach for output [b00689d]. Foundation laid, commit [39461ce] removed the use of strings as an intermediate container for content. This forced several changes to existing tests, causing them to use overrides to inject a `ByteArrayOutputStream` to capture the output for inspection.

Moving Downstream

This last set of changes left me well positioned to implement the various aspects of the output. Commit [99cb54b] introduced an effective but somewhat awkward test to verify that `System.out` was used for normal output. I call it awkward because of the use of the `copiedToOutput` variable that needed checking in the override of `retrieve()`, shown in Listing 14-7. This amounted to a hand-rolled mock. If I left out the flag, I would have no guarantee that `copyToOutput()` was called and therefore that its assertion had been evaluated.

Listing 14-7: *Effective but awkward test with hand-rolled mock to verify that* `System.out` *is used for output*

```
public void testRetrieve_StandardOutput()
    throws IOException, URISyntaxException {
  final String expectedContent = "This should go to stdout";
  Target sut = new Target(EXAMPLE_URI, false) {
    boolean copiedToOutput = false;

    @Override
    public void retrieve()
        throws IOException, URISyntaxException {
      super.retrieve();
      assertThat(copiedToOutput, is(true));
    }

    @Override
    protected void retrieveResponse()
        throws IOException, URISyntaxException {
      setResponse(
        WebRetrieverTest.createMockResponse(expectedContent));
    }

    @Override
    protected void copyToOutput(
        InputStream content, OutputStream output)
        throws IOException {
      assertThat(System.out, is(output));
      copiedToOutput = true;
    }
  };

  sut.retrieve();
}
```

The following commit, [f89bf38], refactors the anonymous inner class to an explicit nested class and turns it into a spy rather than a mock. This yields a nicer-looking test as well as a reusable spy for the other output variations (Listing 14-8).

Listing 14-8: *Cleaned up version of the test in Listing 14-7 showing a cleaner testing style and preparing for reuse in upcoming variations*

```
public void testRetrieve_StandardOutput()
    throws IOException, URISyntaxException {
  OutputSpyTarget sut =
    new OutputSpyTarget(EXAMPLE_URI, false);

  sut.retrieve();

  OutputStream outputStream = sut.getOutputStream();
  assertThat(outputStream, is(notNullValue()));
  assertThat(System.out, is(outputStream));
}

class OutputSpyTarget extends Target {
  OutputStream outputStream = null;

  public OutputSpyTarget(String URI, boolean writeToFile)
      throws URISyntaxException {
    super(URI, writeToFile);
  }

  @Override
  protected void retrieveResponse()
      throws IOException, URISyntaxException {
    setResponse(WebRetrieverTest.createMockResponse(""));
  }

  @Override
  protected void copyToOutput(
        InputStream content, OutputStream output)
      throws IOException {
    outputStream = output;
  }

  public OutputStream getOutputStream() {
    return outputStream;
  }
}
```

The remainder of the commits use the `OutputSpyTarget` to verify that it writes to a file and that it fails when no file path is given.

Retrospective

WebRetriever has reached a functional state with a couple of extra perks over its more mature predecessor `curl`, at least for the implemented features. It can default a scheme, and it automatically follows HTTP-based redirects. The latter could be seen as a liability if you want to use it to diagnose redirect behaviors, but for most content purposes it helps. As I left it, it works as developed if you do the Maven build and invoke it as a JAR.

Its functionality falls short of `curl` by a long shot, but as a demonstration of testing techniques that would get tedious. I have tested a few error conditions, but many remain.

From a software design perspective, it went through some fairly ugly and chaotic intermediate forms, but it is shaping up reasonably. At times, it tested the ability of IntelliJ to refactor unassisted.

I am not crazy about the arguments being handled in the `URIs` parameter of `WebRetriever.retrieve()`. The argument parsing—generously described as parsing—uses a simplistic approach that will not scale, but for a single option it suffices. Moving forward with other options, I would use something like the Apache Commons CLI library.[4]

It seems likely that a `TargetSet` might hold the list of `Target`s to be retrieved and possibly be the container for the global options, while options specific to an individual URI would live with the `Target`. Additionally, the error handling should be strengthened.

But as far as the main point of the exercise went, a demonstration of the use of testing techniques, it covered a lot of ground. First of all, I showed how to apply the techniques in a test-driven manner using a statically typed language. I used an understanding of what testable code looks like to craft tests that exploited the seams I was about to create and used my refactoring phase while the tests were green to position the code for better testability. Of the chapters on the testing implementation patterns, I used techniques from all but Chapter 13.

---

4. http://commons.apache.org/proper/commons-cli/

Chapter 15

Legacy JavaScript

Michael Feathers defines legacy code as code without tests [WEwLC]. JavaScript and other dynamic languages benefit from tests by exercising a wider range of the dynamic behaviors that sometimes make them behave in unanticipated ways. Open-source projects benefit from tests so that multiple contributors can make changes without each having to be intimately familiar with all behaviors.

In contrast, open-source JavaScript projects without tests survive through simplicity or a small number of immersed maintainers, and often both. Increasingly, open-source JavaScript projects include tests, but some very useful and popular projects remain without them.

The jQuery Timepicker Addon[1] by Trent Richardson is one such project. The Timepicker Addon injects time selection into the jQuery UI Datepicker.[2] As you might expect, this allows the selection of times along with dates. It goes well beyond a simple time drop-down menu, however, supporting formatting, time zones, sliders, multiple fields, ranges, constraints, and more. Fortunately, the project includes very thorough documentation with examples, making the task of testing it easier. The project may be used under either GPL or MIT licenses. Trent has wanted to add testing to the project for some time and has eagerly supported this effort and incorporated it into the distribution.

---

1. The project page with documentation and examples can be found at http:// trentrichardson.com/examples/timepicker/, with the source code at http://github .com/trentrichardson/jQuery-Timepicker-Addon.

2. http://jqueryui.com/datepicker/

You can find my fork of the original project at https://github.com/ srvance/jQuery-Timepicker-Addon, which is the repository containing the hash references for this chapter. The commits referenced in the chapter are on the "dev" branch of the repository; this is where Trent requests work to be submitted. As with Chapter 14, I have omitted practices—such as a Grunt build, jslint or jshint, and code coverage— that I would use in a more production-oriented context. I used IntelliJ, with JavaScript intentions enabled, in order to leverage the refactoring support it provides. This also gives some level of static analysis to catch questionable usages. I left the Chrome browser running on a different monitor, using the LivePage[3] plug-in to continuously reload the Jasmine[4] spec runner for the project.

Getting Started

Testing an existing piece of software holds a different set of challenges from testing something you are writing, particularly if it is of any size. The Timepicker Addon had just over 2100 lines of code when I started.

   You first need to choose where to start. Testable entities—functions in JavaScript—that have few or no dependencies, provide you a way to start with something simpler—a way to get a foothold—and work your way up the chain. The first commit, of course, was just setting up the test framework [72007f6].

   I chose to start with a series of top-level private functions within the immediately invoked function expression (IIFE) that wraps every well-written jQuery plugin. But the functions were private, so I had to decide how to expose them for testing. In JavaScript, things are generally either hidden or not, rarely in between. However, some programmers use naming conventions to designate exposed functions as private. Trent used an underscore to mark some functions as private. I followed his lead. Listing 15-1 shows the relevant subset of the IIFE and the technique I used to access the functions.

---

3. https://chrome.google.com/webstore/detail/livepage/ pilnojpmdoofaelbinaeodfpjheijkbh?hl=en

4. http://pivotal.github.io/jasmine/

Listing 15-1: *Exposing private functions in an IIFE for testability*

```
(function($) {
  var extendRemove = function(target, props) { ... };
  var isEmptyObject = function(obj) { ... };
  var convert24to12 = function(hour) { ... };
  var detectSupport = function(timeFormat) { ... };

  $.timepicker._util = {
    _extendRemove: extendRemove,
    _isEmptyObject: isEmptyObject,
    _convert24to12: convert24to12,
    _detectSupport: detectSupport
  };
})(jQuery);
```

Exposing these internal methods by making them underscore-prefixed methods of an underscore-prefixed object on the `timepicker` let me access them from tests like

```
$.timepicker._util._extendRemove(target, props);
```

for very easy testing. The initial 19 tests, through commit [d0245b6], fixed two bugs and enabled safe, test-protected simplification of other code.

DOMination

The function `selectLocalTimezone()`, only six lines long and shown in Listing 15-2, forced me to bring in some additional techniques. This function sets the selected value of a selection list representing time zone choices to that of the current or specified time zone. This small piece of code uses jQuery to operate on the DOM.

Listing 15-2: *A small method using jQuery to operate on the DOM. The* `timezone_select` *property is supposed to be a jQuery collection referencing a* `<select>` *tag.*

```
var selectLocalTimezone = function(tp_inst, date) {
  if (tp_inst && tp_inst.timezone_select) {
    var now = date || new Date();
    tp_inst.timezone_select.val(-now.getTimezoneOffset());
  }
};
```

I had originally set up the Jasmine spec runner to include jasmine-jquery,[5] confusing it with jasmine-fixture.[6] My next action was to correct that [f018316]. The jasmine-fixture module lets me define DOM fixtures based on jQuery selector syntax that get cleaned up automatically. I used it to set up a structure like Timepicker expected for the operation of the method and tested to ensure that the right value was selected [34e2ee2], partially shown in Listing 15-3.

Listing 15-3: *A test using jasmine-fixture to set up the DOM as expected*

```
describe('selectLocalTimezone', function() {
  var timepicker,
    timezoneOffset,
    defaultTimezoneOffset;

  beforeEach(function() {
    timepicker = {
      timezone_select: affix('select')
    };
    var now = new Date();
      timezoneOffset = String(-now.getTimezoneOffset());
      defaultTimezoneOffset = String(timezoneOffset - 60);
    timepicker.timezone_select.affix('option')
      .text(defaultTimezoneOffset);
    timepicker.timezone_select.affix('option')
      .text(timezoneOffset);
    timepicker.timezone_select.affix('option')
      .text(timezoneOffset + 60);
  });

  it('should select the current timezone with a valid ' +
      'timezone_select and a date', function() {
    util._selectLocalTimezone(timepicker, new Date());

    expect(timepicker.timezone_select.val())
      .toBe(timezoneOffset);
  });
});
```

---

5. https://github.com/velesin/jasmine-jquery
6. https://github.com/searls/jasmine-fixture

On Toothpaste and Testing

I often call the approach of bottom-up testing **toothpaste testing**. You start from the bottom and slowly squeeze your way to the top. It goes hand in hand with **toothpaste refactoring**, which follows the same pattern and is supported by toothpaste testing.

Toothpaste refactoring provides an alternative to the legacy rescue approach of using characterization tests to drive down from the top. Both have their places. I have seen many occasions in which seemingly beneficial refactorings—such as adding dependency injection or changing signatures—percolate down through the call hierarchy only to be stopped by some strange construct. Additionally, top-down refactoring runs the risk of going long periods of time without your testing safety net, as you break layer after layer, changing its shape.

Working from the bottom up requires some level of confidence—or at least optimism—that the lower-level entities are valuable to test. You will also have to do a lot of reverse engineering of intent. But if you think the overall design and implementation are sound and just missing tests, the toothpaste approach works well.

The other utility functions to parse the date and time strings are a little more complicated, so I decided to turn my attention to the public `$.timepicker` functions. Starting with `timezoneOffsetNumber()`, testing uncovered a seeming discrepancy of intent against the comments [83b6840].

Moving to `timezoneOffsetString()` [7bc2133] uncovered an imbalanced range validation for which the upper boundary of the range was checked but not the lower value. I enhanced the documentation to explain the "magic" numbers in the code that corresponded to the highest and lowest actual time zone offsets in minutes. Once test protection was in place, I was also able to eliminate more "magic" numbers to simplify zero-padding the digits in the result string.

Testing the `log()` function triggered the first use of Jasmine's built-in spy capability [1adc385]. Timepicker's logging is a thin wrapper that makes sure that the console exists before trying to log through it. I believe this accounts for a Firefox compatibility issue. For testing, I had to determine whether the requested message was output with and without `window.console` being defined. Technically, you cannot prove that the function did not output the message. I relied on the white-box knowledge that it uses `console.log()` to verify that it did not call that method. Fortunately, you can spy on these kinds of "system" functions as easily as any other function.

Covering `timezoneAdjust()` with tests [b23be92] allowed the safe simplification of the computation in [af26afc]. I tested this function somewhat reluctantly. The JavaScript `Date` object seems incomplete with respect to its time zone handling. Its API omits the ability to change the time zone. The constructor sets it to the browser's time zone, from which point it remains read-only. Methods like this one try to compensate by adjusting the minutes by the change in offset. This allows most date math operations to yield useful results in a pragmatic way, but the underlying principle is flawed from an international date- and time-handling perspective. However, JavaScript has this limitation, and the rest of us need to live with it.

While the `handleRange()` function is complex, the value of the other range functions is simply to call it in the right way. I tested the callers independently using the spy feature [9254a37]. Listing 15-4 shows an example of this usage. I refactored the tests into a subgroup in [afb4c98] and deferred `handleRange()` itself by adding a placeholder [f363202].

Listing 15-4: *Using a spy to verify the value added by a function that simply calls another function with the right arguments*

```
var startTime = $('<p>start</p>'),
    endTime = $('<p>end</p>'),
    options = {};

beforeEach(function() {
  spyOn($.timepicker, 'handleRange');
});

it('timeRange calls handleRange the right way', function() {
  $.timepicker.timeRange(startTime, endTime, options);

  expect($.timepicker.handleRange)
    .toHaveBeenCalledWith('timepicker',
      startTime, endTime, options);
});
```

Ignoring the explicit documentation in front of my face, I initially passed strings as the `startTime` and `endTime` parameters, but fortunately IntelliJ corrected me.

Scaling Up

One of the bigger challenges in taming legacy code is the size and scope of the existing functions. Larger functions have more dependencies and more complicated logic. You first need to write characterization tests to capture the intent before refactoring to smaller, more focused functions. The functions that I deferred so far fall in that category. I had run out of simple functions and needed to forge ahead.

The next most complicated functions were the date and time parsing utility functions deferred earlier. Of the two remaining functions, `splitDateTime()` and `parseDateInternal()`, `splitDateTime()` was the easier. For one, `parseDateInternal()` calls `splitDateTime()`, and it also calls other functions of the `datepicker`, both original and overridden.

As with the other utility functions, I started by exposing it through the `_util` namespace I added [ff99363]. Testing the happy path and a couple variations ended up being straightforward. The daunting part was the error path. The code contained a cryptic comment about leveraging the format of an error message as a hack (it said so in the code!) to avoid replicating parsing logic. However, I could not see where in the `try` block such an exception could be generated in order to test it. For the time being, I left a `TODO` to mark the loose end.

I chose to continue to `parseDateTimeInternal()`, despite not having tested the rather complex collaborator functions it relies on. Fortunately, the intent of the collaborators seemed clear, and the returns from each passed directly to the return result without additional manipulation. I only needed to understand how to pass the right parameters to trigger the desired result.

The first two tests exercised the happy path variations. I chose to throw in microseconds for the time-parsing path, which made the setup a little more complex.

The error path test introduced a new Jasmine feature, the `toThrow()` matcher [1cc967a]. To use this matcher (Listing 15-5), you need to structure your expectation a little differently.

Listing 15-5: *Use of Jasmine's* `toThrow()` *matcher to verify an exception error path*

```
it('should throw an exception if it cannot parse the time',
    function() {
  var inputDateString = '4/17/2008 11:22:33';

  expect(function() {
    $.timepicker._util._parseDateTimeInternal(
      dateFormat, 'q', inputDateString, undefined, undefined
    );
  }).toThrow('Wrong time format');
});
```

Instead of providing a value to `expect()`, you provide a function that Jasmine invokes, capturing and storing the exception for matching.

Testing the error path found a bug. The underlying parsing used by the collaborator `$.datepicker.parseTime()` returns `false` if it cannot parse the time. However, the implementation tests the return from this function against `null` using the `===` operator. If you are not familiar with them, the `==` and `===` operators in JavaScript are similar, except that the latter one also checks the type of its operands while the former happily coerces values' types to see if there is a match. While `null` is **falsey**[7] in JavaScript and would evaluate false with the `==` operator, the strict equivalence comparison sees them as different. As a result, the comparison never triggered the exception. Simply changing the equality test (`parsedTime === null`) to a logical negation (`!parsedTime`) fixed the problem [c264915].

With test protection, I could refactor `parseDateTime-Internal()` to simplify it [353ff5e]. The existing `timeString` variable was unused, so I used it where its initializer had been duplicated to be more intent revealing. I flipped the if-else statement so that it started with the positive condition rather than the negation. This allowed me to flatten some of the nested conditionals by handling the no-time situation with a guard condition that returns early. The flattened function is much cleaner to read.

---

7. In JavaScript, falsey values are `false`, `null`, `undefined`, `0`, `NaN`, and the empty string. All other values are **truthy**, including empty objects and arrays.

I wanted to do a couple more cleanups before leaving the time-utility functions. The `splitDateTime()` function returned a two-element array consisting of the date and time strings by construction. The `parseDateTimeInternal()` function introduced intermediate variables to provide intent-revealing names to the elements of the returned array. I decided to turn the return array into an object so that the intent-revealing names were built into the return [353ff5e]. This allowed the removal of the intermediate variable [5109082].

The beginning two variable initializations of `splitDateTime()` struck me as verbose and highly similar. They determined a property by giving the passed settings, if defined, priority over the Timepicker defaults. Commit [11a2545] refactored the initialization logic into a common function `computeEffectiveSetting()`. Of course, the new function needed to be directly tested [ea7babe], but I left all of the testing variations of `splitDateTime()` because they also represent important behavioral facets.

Software Archeology

The difficulty of testing the error path of `splitDateTime()` and the fact that I could not figure out where the exception supposedly came from bothered me. It was time for an archeological expedition into the project's history.

Searching back, I discovered that the error handling was added two years prior as part of a different function [4496926]. I also noticed that the body of the `try` block called a collaborator that was no longer involved in the present day code. About a year ago, it was refactored into its current function [e7c7d40], but the `try` block still called the collaborator. Finally, I found the code from ten months ago that replaced the original implementation with the current one [b838a21]. The current code could not throw the exception that it was catching and trying to process. As a result, I could delete the entire error handling block, the `try/catch` surrounding the implementation [6adc077], the placeholder to test the error path that no longer existed. This allowed me in turn to eliminate two now-unused parameters to `splitDateTime()`.

Retrospective

As of this writing, I have not finished testing the Timepicker Addon. I have pushed 37 commits to my fork of the project. I have created two pull requests, of which Trent has accepted and merged one to the dev branch. I plan to finish covering the code, fixing and refactoring as I find things.

In this example, we saw a different approach to testing. Bringing untested code under test has a different flow from test driving a new project. Even though this project was pretty well written to start, I found and fixed bugs, uncovered ambiguous intent, unearthed vestigial code, cleaned up warnings, and improved readability.

This project showed some of the differences working in a dynamic language and with a different flavor of testing framework. The testing required the use of a variety of matchers for both result and error verification, as well as the use of spies for behavioral verification. At times, I thought I would need some of the other spy behaviors, such as the ability to return a specified value, but I was proven wrong by commit time. Perhaps most interestingly, I started to explore the techniques used to test JavaScript that interacts with the DOM by using Jasmine extensions to create automatically torn down DOM fixtures.

Bibliography

[ASD] Martin, Robert C. *Agile Software Development: Principles, Patterns, and Practices*. Upper Saddle River, NJ: Prentice Hall, 2003.

[AT] Crispin, Lisa, and Janet Gregory. *Agile Testing: A Practical Guide for Testers and Agile Teams*. Boston, MA: Addison-Wesley, 2009.

[CC08] Martin, Robert C. *Clean Code: A Handbook of Agile Software Craftsmanship*. Upper Saddle River, NJ: Prentice Hall, 2009.

[CC11] Martin, Robert C. *The Clean Coder: A Code of Conduct for Professional Programmers*. Upper Saddle River, NJ: Prentice Hall, 2011.

[DP] Gamma, Erich, Richard Helm, Ralph Johnson, and John Vlissides. *Design Patterns: Elements of Reusable Object-Oriented Software*. Reading, MA: Addison-Wesley, 1995.

[GOOS] Freeman, Steve, and Nat Pryce. *Growing Object-Oriented Software, Guided by Tests*. Boston, MA: Addison-Wesley, 2010.

[JCIP] Goetz, Brian, with Tim Peierls, Joshua Bloch, Joseph Bowbeer, David Holmes, and Doug Lea. *Java Concurrency in Practice*. Boston, MA: Addison-Wesley, 2006.

[JTGP] Crockford, Douglas. *JavaScript: The Good Parts*. Sebastopol, CA: O'Reilly Media, Inc., 2008.

[KOR85] Korel, B., and J. Laski. "A Tool for Data Flow Oriented Program Testing." *ACM Softfair Proceedings* (Dec 1985): 35–37.

[LAS83] Laski, Janusz W., and Bogdan Korel. "A Data Flow Oriented Program Testing Strategy." *IEEE Transactions on Software Engineering SE-9 (3)*: 347–354.

[MEC] Meyers, Scott. *More Effective C++: 35 New Ways to Improve Your Programs and Designs*. Reading, MA: Addison-Wesley, 1996.

[PBP] Conway, Damian. *Perl Best Practices*. Sebastopol, CA: O'Reilly Media, Inc., 2005.

[REF] Fowler, Martin. *Refactoring: Improving the Design of Existing Code*. Reading, MA: Addison-Wesley, 1999.

[RTP] Kerievsky, Joshua. *Refactoring to Patterns*. Boston, MA: Addison-Wesley, 2005.

[SD] Yourdon, Edward, and Larry L. Constantine. *Structured Design: Fundamentals of a Discipline of Computer Program and Systems Design*. Englewood Cliffs, NJ: Prentice Hall, 1979.

[WEwLC] Feathers, Michael C. *Working Effectively with Legacy Code*. Upper Saddle River, NJ: Prentice Hall, 2005.

[XPE] Beck, Kent. *Extreme Programming Explained: Embrace Change*. Boston, MA: Addison-Wesley, 2000.

[XPI] Jeffries, Ron, Ann Anderson, and Chet Hendrickson. *Extreme Programming Installed*. Boston, MA: Addison-Wesley, 2001.

[xTP] Meszaros, Gerard. *xUnit Test Patterns: Refactoring Test Code*. Boston, MA: Addison-Wesley, 2007.

Index

FREE
Online Edition